ON PAPER

CW01669827

HAYWARD GALLERY PUBLISHING

Arts Council Collection

Foreword

Jill Constantine,
Ann Jones

For much of its 2,000-year history, paper has been a precious commodity, highly valued by artists and used sparingly. It was only after it became industrially produced in the nineteenth century that the cost fell dramatically, and by the mid twentieth century it had become a cheap, easy-to-discard material. Now we are well into the digital era, and it is easy to question the relevance of paper in modern life. We use e-tickets to travel, read e-books and e-newspapers, and emails have long replaced most letter writing; yet, as Ian Sansom points out in his essay to this publication, we are still reliant on paper in our everyday lives. His long list of paper items still to be digitally replaced includes wrapping paper, cereal packets, teabags, fireworks, tissues, emery boards, takeaway coffee cups, birthday cards and passports. Undeniably, many artists would struggle without paper: first ideas are often worked out on paper and, as this exhibition demonstrates, drawing is only one of myriad ways that paper can be used in art.

A quick search through the Arts Council Collection database proves that over half the works incorporate paper in some way. Although a large number of these works are photographs, prints and drawings, this is still a substantial part of the Collection. A more detailed search reveals that these works also include sculptures, books, paintings and collages, and that the artists have usually chosen paper for very specific reasons: some because it was the material most suited to their work and others for the ease with which this material could be sculpted, torn and generally transformed.

During 2016 and 2017 the Arts Council Collection toured *Drawn from Life: People on Paper*, an exhibition exploring the development of figurative drawing, spanning over a century of British art. Now, with *On Paper*, our aim is to look beyond the mark-making of drawing and consider the very material itself. This new exhibition shows how paper does not only belong to drawings and collage, but is also used to create three-dimensional objects, such as Karla Black's delicate and sensuous hanging sculptures made from sugar paper, hair gel and chalk, Lesley Foxcroft's two-tone corrugated bricks and Gareth Jones's cape made from cloakroom tickets. Other artists included in the exhibition have exploited the fragility of paper as a material that can be easily burnt, cut or torn. Roger Ackling, Tim Davies and Cornelia Parker have all burnt parts of their paper works, while Simon Periton has delicately cut the foil paper in his piece *SP* (p. 65), though not with his *Scalpel* (p. 66), which has ironically been made from paper itself. Collage is perhaps the most well-known form of cut paper, and Ian Breakwell, Eduardo Paolozzi, John Stezaker and Tony Swain have cut and pasted works using newsprint, postcards and photographs. Paper is extremely versatile, as is seen in works by Anna Barriball, Langlands & Bell and Wolfgang Tillmans, where it has been rubbed, embossed and folded, further exploring its tactile nature. In his film *Rosebud*, James Richards includes close-ups of art books found in a library in Tokyo featuring a selection of illustrations that have been partially scraped and sand-papered, in order to comply with Japanese censorship laws.

For some of the artists in *On Paper*, the choice of a particular type of paper is an important consideration when making their work: the precision of Kenneth Martin and Bridget Riley's works is reflected in their preference for graph paper; Jason Coburn creates a conflicting play between his scrawled words and the Ministry of Defence headed paper on which they are written; the wilting daffodils of Margaret Mellis's pastel drawing seem to droop into the corners of a torn open envelope, while Prunella Clough's ink line winds its way over the troughs of the corrugated card. Finally, Derek Boshier, Kate Davis and Tania Kovats have chosen to draw paper itself in the form of a theatre ticket, a museum postcard and books, transforming the subject into the object itself.

It has been a pleasure to witness the enthusiasm shown by the many contributors to this timely exhibition, particularly Ian Sansom who, having previously explored in-depth the history of paper and its many forms and functions, has written an informative and extremely enjoyable essay for this publication. Our thanks go to him for his contribution.

Chris McCabe, Librarian at the National Poetry Library at the Southbank Centre, kindly introduced us to poet Joey Connolly, who has written a number of beautifully sensitive new poems inspired by the 49 works in the exhibition. One of these poems, *Forty-nine Moments for the Substrate*, is included in this publication.

We are grateful to Director of Visual Arts at the British Council Collection Emma Dexter, and her team, for once again facilitating the exhibition by lending us six works from their collection. The exhibition will travel to many galleries around the country: Perth Museum and Art Gallery; Gallery Oldham; Inverness Museum and Art Gallery; Oriel Wrecsam; Glynn Vivian Art Gallery, Swansea; Victoria Art Gallery, Bath; and Thelma Hulbert Gallery, Honiton, and we look forward to working with these venues.

We should also like to record our thanks to members of our Collection team, particularly Grace Beaumont, Rachel Graves and Natalie Rudd for their illuminating texts on a number of the works included in this publication; Marketing Officer Affly Johnson; and Collection Assistants Kate Devine and Louise Smith, for providing invaluable administrative support. Our thanks are also due to Andy Craig and Joshua Dowson from our technical team for their care and attention to detail, as well as the Hayward Gallery Registrars Charlotte Booth, Alison Maun and Imogen Winter. Last but by no means least, we are grateful to Diana Adell and Rebecca Fortey from Hayward Gallery Publishing, and ARPA Studio, who have together produced this delightful publication to accompany the exhibition.

Jill Constantine, Director, and Ann Jones, Curator, Arts Council Collection

11

On Paper

Ian Sansom

We are all paper people: we are all made of paper.

Paper money has made our economies and determines our destinies. Paper maps have divided our land. Paper laws have propped up our governments and paper books have shaped our minds.

Despite the obvious encroachments of the digital, we all still use so much paper – to note, to register, to measure, to account for, to classify, authorise, endorse and generally to tot up, gee up and make good our lives – that it would be a gargantuan undertaking to provide a full history of all the paper in just one life on one day, never mind in one city on one day, or in the life of one nation.

Fortunate for us, then, that James Joyce undertook just such a task in his novel *Ulysses*, thus saving us the bother. One of the great constructions of the human imagination, *Ulysses*, published in 1922, is nothing if not a vast paper palace, made up of bits of posters, pamphlets, sandwich boards and boot blacking ads; it is also a book literally composed from paper scraps. 'I make notes on the backs of advertisements,' Joyce told a friend in 1917. He also made much use of waistcoat-pocket-sized pieces of paper, large enough to make multiple memos-to-self about Epps's cocoa, Bushmills whiskey, Guinness, Cantrell & Cochrane's ginger ale, Pears soap and Plumtree's potted meat, all of which feature largely and exuberantly throughout the novel.

Like Joyce – indeed like all writers and artists – we are paper omnivores. We devour it: any kind, from anywhere. During the course of this week alone I have fingered and handled not only books, newspapers and magazines, but also files, agendas, programmes, dry cleaning tickets, cinema tickets, parking tickets, boarding cards, feedback forms, school reports, bills, invoices and packaging of all kinds, and my pockets, as always, are stuffed full with train tickets, money and receipts, so much so that sometimes at night I simply shake the contents out onto the floor, creating a paper shower that soon becomes a drift which eventually, if allowed, would overcome first my bedroom, then my house, and then finally my life. This brings to mind the famous American Collyer brothers, Homer and Langley, whose brownstone on Fifth Avenue in New York was filled from floor to ceiling with a lifetime's junk, and who eventually died in squalor and infamy in 1947, with the police removing over 100 tons of garbage from their home. Homer had starved to death, while Langley had been crushed in one of the booby-trapped newspaper tunnels of his own construction.

For better and for worse, then, paper remains our daily bread, the fuel of our everyday existence, the substratum of our lives, our absolute all-time favourite self-extending prosthetic technology and device. It enables and represents the best of us, and the worst. It is the very essence of life and also – as the works in this exhibition so amply demonstrate – of art.

Of course, not all art takes place on paper. And not all art on paper is what we might call paper art. And some paper art may not conform to traditional ideas of what art should be. The Italian artist Lucio Fontana, for example, was famous for making cuts and punctures in his canvases. Gordon Matta-Clark specialised in making slits and cuts in surfaces of every kind, including paper, while Martin Creed's *Work No. 88* is simply *A sheet of A4 paper crumpled into a ball.* Tom Friedman's *1000 Hours of Staring* is a plain white piece of paper that has been stared at. For a very long time.

But these are only some of the more obvious examples of the role of paper in art. It is in fact possible to argue that the development of *all* modern art derives from what the American critic Clement Greenberg called in 1958 the 'pasted-paper revolution'. According to Greenberg, the use of paper collage in the early twentieth century by Cubist artists such as Georges Braque and Pablo Picasso liberated art from being merely decorative or an attempt simply to illustrate reality.

In the 1920s, for example, Joan Miró decided that his aim was to 'assassinate painting'. Miró's first, rather half-hearted, act of rebellion was to stick postcards on canvas, but in 1933 he began cutting images of machines and tools from catalogues and sticking them to large sheets of Ingres paper. He then began to use the outline shapes formed by these cut-outs as models for his paintings: this was his revelation, his big breakthrough. Released from the constraints both of self-expression and of spontaneity, Miró had found an unexpected route to the vague symbolic language that characterises his later work, with its unique constellations of shapes, signs and lines. In order to find the true language and expression of his art, Miró had to start with scissors and paper.

Henri Matisse devoted the final few years of his life almost entirely to cutting shapes from paper that had previously been painted with gouache and were subsequently pasted down. These paper collages inaugurated a new phase of his career: 'une seconde vie', a second life. 'The cut-out paper', he explained in a letter in 1948, 'allows me to draw in colour. It is a simplification.' Paper allowed Matisse to get back to basics, to return to what mattered: 'I have needed all that time to reach the stage where I can say what I want to say,' he wrote, and he could only say it through paper.

Like Miró and Matisse, the artists represented in *On Paper* use paper not only as a medium but also as the very matter of their art: it is the subject and the object, the means of production and the artefact produced. There are extraordinary examples of collage in the exhibition – from Eduardo Paolozzi's *A Logical Picture of Facts is a Thought (3) Tractatus '21-22'* (p. 59) to John Stezaker's *Mask LXIV* (p. 69). There is also paper burnt, torn and otherwise transformed – Cornelia Parker's *Meteorite Lands on Wormwood Scrubs* (pp. 60–61) and Roger Ackling's *Five Hour Cloud Drawing* (p. 25). And there is paper viewed as a sculptural object – Karla Black's *Unused To* (pp. 30–31) and Wolfgang Tillmans's *paper drop (London)* (pp. 72–73). Many of these artists address directly what the art historian Martin Kemp calls 'die Materialfrage', the materials question: how far does the material available to an artist determine the nature of their work? What is the relationship between the thing made, and the thing being used to make it?

Brian Griffiths's *Ron* (pp. 38–39) recreates a giant computer made entirely out of cardboard: the work makes the familiar strange and also perhaps questions the relationship between the hi-tech and the homemade. Simon Periton's punky paper cut-outs (p. 65) are a distinctively modern British take on the ancient art of paper-cutting, an art form which spans the globe – from Japanese *kirigami* and Chinese *jian zhi*, to Spanish *papel picado* and Polish *wycinanki*. Linder's collages push the DIY aesthetic even further, recycling and reusing paper for purposes previously unimagined (pp. 50–51). Anna Barriball's *Window* (p. 29) uses paper to reveal textures unseen. And Bridget Riley's drawing *Structural and Tonal Movements in Opposition* beautifully illustrates the common working out of ideas on paper.

So various and so inventive is the engagement of these artists with paper that we might forget that paper's ubiquity as a plaything and as a tool is a relatively recent phenomenon. Until the beginning of the nineteenth century, paper was handmade, and therefore expensive. Apprentice artists tended to use erasable drawing tablets in order to learn their craft, and even established artists were not likely to waste paper on mere sketches and drawings. Manufacturers relied on supplies of rags to make their pulp, and it was not until the introduction of the Fourdrinier paper machine in the early decades of the nineteenth century and the advent of wood pulping processes in the 1840s that paper production rapidly increased and paper became omnipresent. The mills began spewing paper into the atmosphere, out onto the streets, into studios, offices and into people's everyday lives. The effect was both suffocating and intoxicating. In a popular engraving from 1862, *The Bill Poster's Dream*, a figure sits slumped like a drunk against a lamp post, exhausted, a glue-pot by his side and examples of his handiwork illuminating the night sky. In an article on 'Bill-Sticking' published in *Household Words* (March 1851), Charles Dickens described the sides of an old warehouse peeling away with layer upon layer of decomposing posters, 'as if they were interminable'.

Interminable, infinite and full of potential – the history of humans working with and on paper is the history of our lives. In the twenty-first century everything that matters to us *still* happens on paper. We are born, and are issued with a birth certificate. We collect more certificates at school, and yet more at work, and when we marry and divorce, and buy a house, and when we die. We are encased and inscribed with deeds and contracts, engrafted into paper, which becomes our artificial skin – and which outlives us. Even in the digital age, paper remains the ghost in our machines, the shadow behind every act of communication. Our most cherished new technologies still resemble the page: the iPad like a jotter; the Kindle like a book; the mobile phone a pocket-diary. The word processing document I am typing into has all the appearance of a sheet of fresh white paper. There are pages, paragraphs and margins. I will 'file' the 'document' in a 'folder'. And lo, by the miracle of email, print and publication, you are reading it now, in black and white, on paper.

Not only for artists, then, but for us all, paper persists – as a resource, as a tool, and as a source of inspiration.

Alfred H. Barr, *Matisse: His Art and His Public* (New York: Museum of Modern Art, 1951)

Alfred Paul Berger, 'James Joyce, Adman', in *James Joyce Quarterly*, 3:1 (Fall 1965)

Charles Dickens, 'Bill-Sticking', in Michael Slater (ed.), *Dickens' Journalism, Volume 2: 'The Amusements of the People' and Other Papers 1834–35* (Columbus: Ohio University Press, 1996)

Jacques Dupin, *Miró* (Paris: Flammarion, 2004)

Clement Greenberg, *The Collected Essays and Criticism, Volume 4: Modernism with a Vengeance, 1957–1969*, ed. John O'Brian (Chicago: University of Chicago Press, 1993)

Dard Hunter, *Papermaking: The History and Technique of an Ancient Craft* (London: Cresset Press, 2nd edn. 1957)

Martin Kemp, *The Science of Art: Optical Themes in Western Art from Brunelleschi to Seurat* (New Haven: Yale University Press, 1990)

Franz Lidz, *Ghosty Men: The Strange but True Story of the Collyer Brothers, New York's Greatest Hoarders* (New York: Bloomsbury, 2003)

19

Forty-nine Moments for the Substrate

Joey Connolly

Moment, n. (3) A turning effect produced by a force acting at a distance on an object.

Substrate, n. (2) The surface or material on or from which an organism lives, grows, or obtains its nourishment.

'…I *felt* the great strength of *the page*: its ability, as a fibrous *surface*, to *deflect* the *point* of my *pen*. The paper, and then *the screen*, as weirdly *reflective*, repelling the ink or the *touch*.' – Bhanu Kapil

Forty-nine sweet lapses
                                        as the substrate
rears up through its foreground
to paw aside the small-talk of convention

and the brute matter of things
insists upon itself. The deft canvas
all the world is impastoed onto

booms and warps in the wallspace
behind the engine room of the faculties.
Forty-nine astringent objections
to the fair & lovely model

of necessity and established order. Forty-
-nine strange hurrahs for the substrate
and the bright matter of things

beats the rhythm of insistence
on the drum of its skin.
Forty-nine gaps in the gap of thought

that things live in, from which the vehicle
bodies forth, scattering its tenor like

cloud, the rich feeling
uncoupling from the error
which begat it. Here. The bright patter of

thought against the rectangle
of skylight above you this Autumn morning,
and the brute matter of the bright

pattern of surface and material
standing amicably by, and the substrate
laps sweetly

at the shore of all this
hall of the material's emanate moment.

Plates

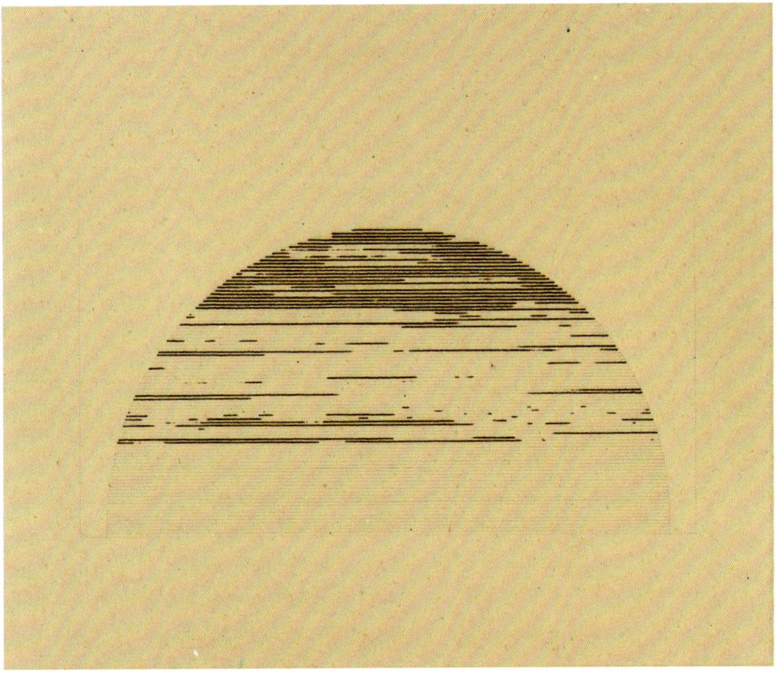

Roger Ackling
Five Hour Cloud Drawing, 1980

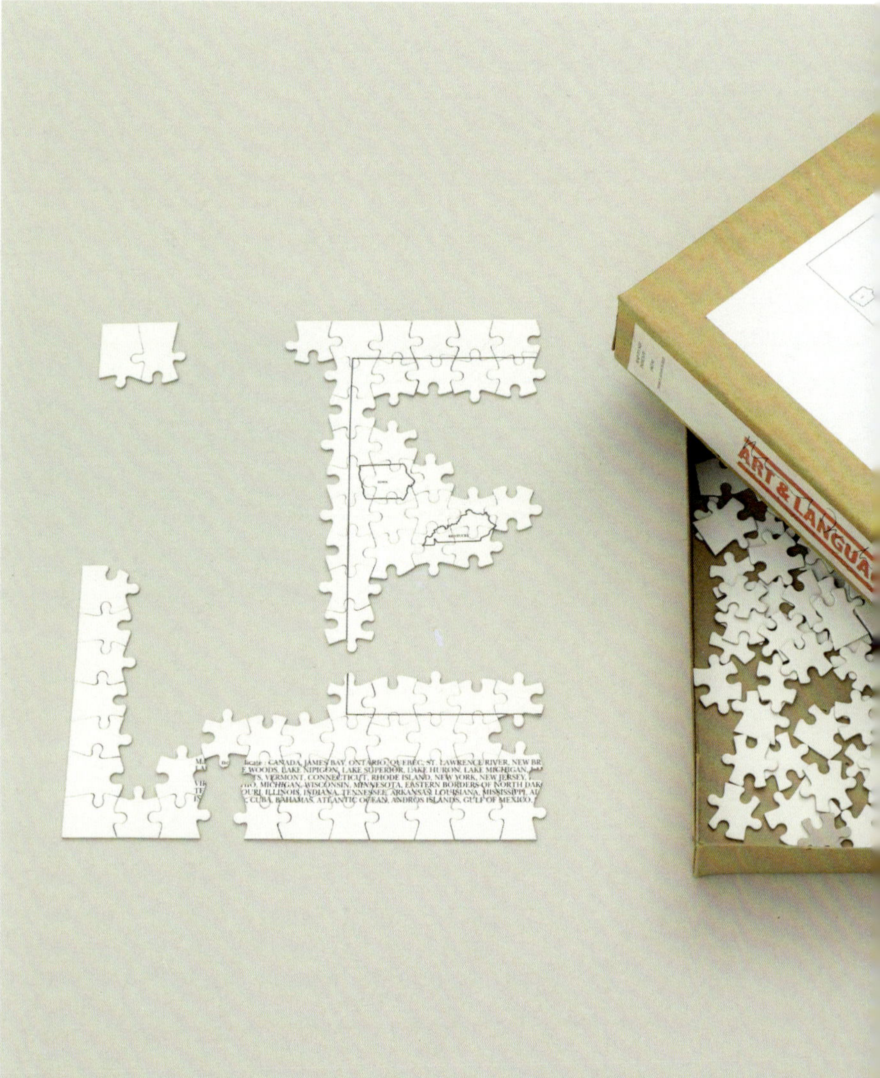
CANADA, JAMES BAY, ONTARIO, QUEBEC, ST. LAWRENCE RIVER, NEW BR
WOODS, LAKE NIPIGON, LAKE SUPERIOR, LAKE HURON, LAKE MICHIGAN,
VERMONT, CONNECTICUT, RHODE ISLAND, NEW YORK, NEW JERSEY,
MICHIGAN, WISCONSIN, MINNESOTA, EASTERN BORDERS OF NORTH DAK
ILLINOIS, INDIANA, TENNESSEE, ARKANSAS, LOUISIANA, MISSISSIPPI,
CUBA, BAHAMAS, ATLANTIC OCEAN, ANDROS ISLANDS, GULF OF MEXICO,
ART & LANGUA

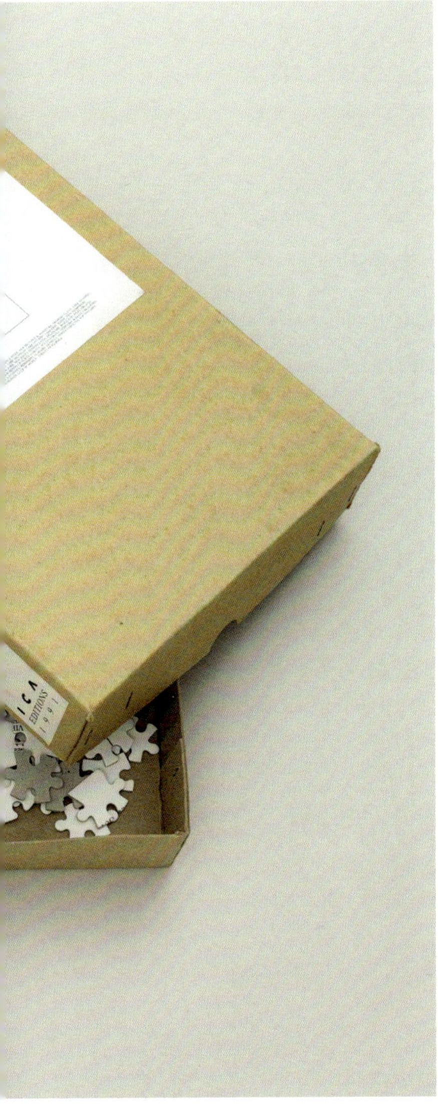

Art & Language
Map to Not Indicate..., 1991

Art & Language are a collective who formed in the late 1960s. Their work encompasses performance, objects, prints and paintings, and aims to challenge the convictions of conventional art practice. Assembled in Coventry, the founding members were Terry Atkinson, Michael Baldwin, David Bainbridge and Harold Hurrell. The critic Charles Harrison and the artists Ian Burn, Joseph Kosuth and Mel Ramsden later became linked to the group, as well as numerous others. *Art-Language* was also the name of their journal, which was dedicated to theoretical and critical discussions on conceptual art. Much of the group's early work relied on detailed exploration of these issues, and was presented in the journal as well as in the gallery space.

Map to Not Indicate... is a multiple in the form of a jigsaw puzzle, kept in an archive box. It is based on an earlier print by the group of the same title (1967), a map which displays only two American states, Iowa and Kentucky. A list below the formation indicates all of the states which have been excluded. The remaining pair are outlined and labelled, drifting like islands in a non-existent sea, thus losing their geographical context. Here, Art & Language play with boundaries, reducing their fabricated map to fragments to be assembled, with no factual resolution.

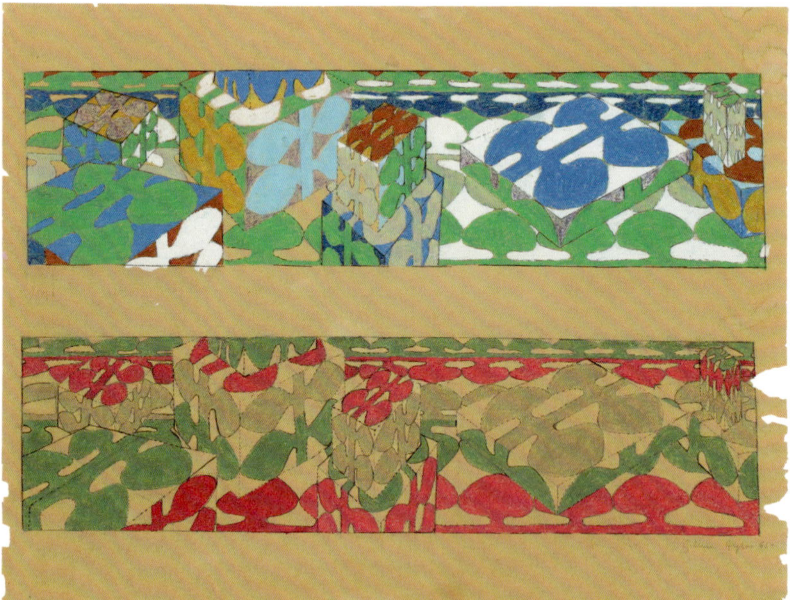

Gillian Ayres
Untitled, 1965

Anna Barriball
Window, 2002

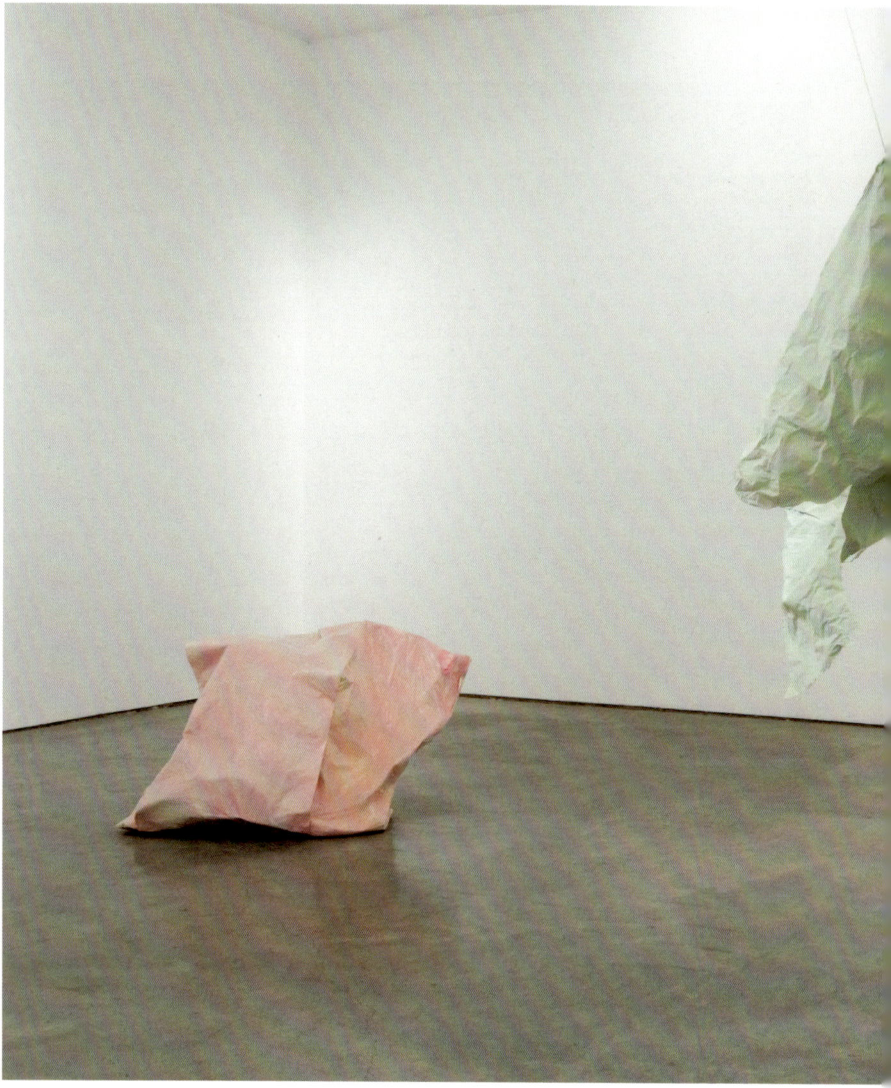

Karla Black
Unused To, 2007

Karla Black combines traditional sculptural materials with more unusual substances such as powder, soap and toothpaste to create large abstract sculptures and installations. Black describes her approach to making as a 'physical exploration into thinking, feeling, communicating and relating, where material experience is prioritised over language as an alternative way to learn and understand'.

Unused To is a delicate two-part sculpture made from a number of essentially formless materials including nail varnish, chalk and hair gel, as well as sugar paper, ribbon and thin sheets of polythene. The everyday materials that Karla Black uses are chosen for their material appearance and colour rather than for any possible metaphorical or associative meanings. As with *Unused To*, the forms that Black creates inhabit their space in a defiantly physical way, often suspended in mid-air as if to greet the viewer at their own level.

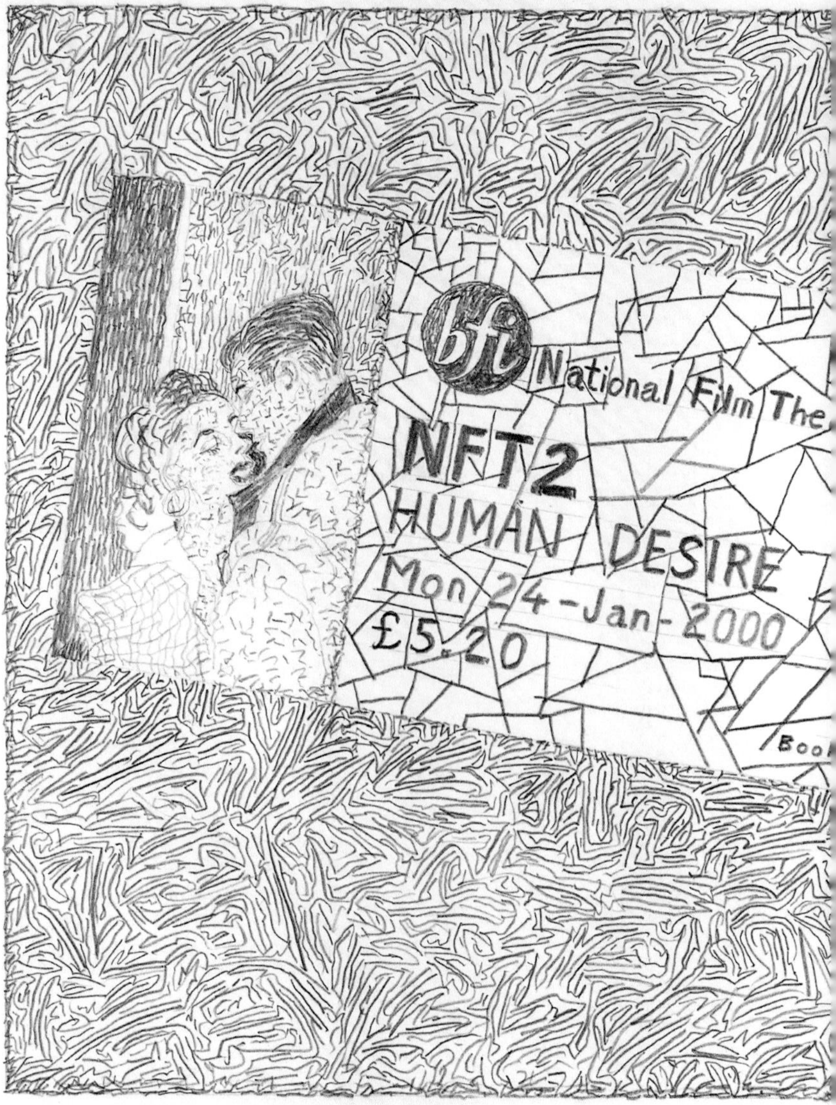
bfi
National Film The
NFT2
HUMAN DESIRE
Mon 24-Jan-2000
£5.20
Boo

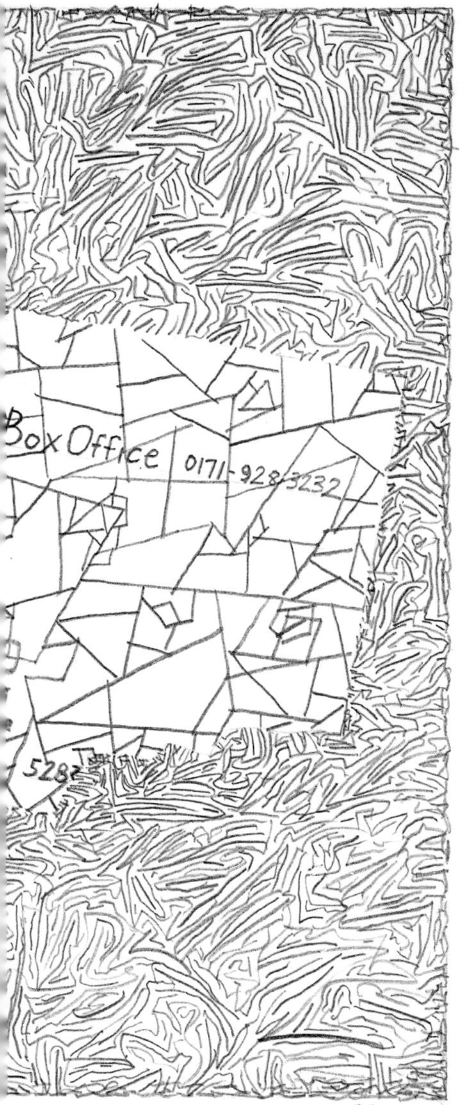

Derek Boshier
National Film Theatre, 2000

Kate Davis
Who is a Woman now? I, 2008

Kate Davis works across a range of media, specifically drawing, collage and sculpture. The subjects in her artworks often reference the human body, and emerge disjointed and distorted. She frequently responds to the aesthetic and political ambiguities of historical artworks and their reception. *Who is a Woman now? I* is a delicate pencil drawing of what seems to be a crumpled postcard, folded in half like a body bent from the waist and flanked with a dense black background. The reproduction bears resemblance to a Willem de Kooning painting from his seminal *Woman* series (1951–53), and the address of the Museum of Modern Art, New York, features along the edge. De Kooning's representations of women were perceived by some to be menacing and objectifying, with their snarling expressions painted with wild brushstrokes, leading to accusations of misogyny. Davis's depiction of the ruined image suggests protest from her standpoint as a female artist working today.

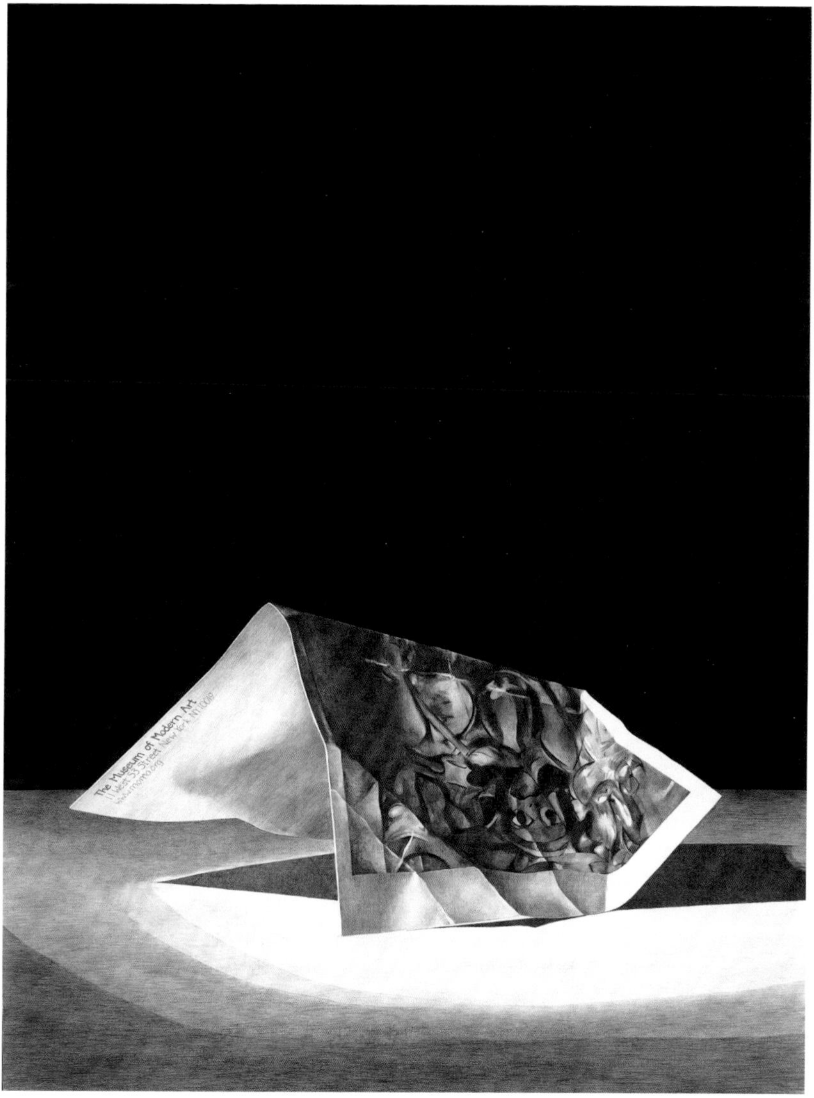
The Museum of Modern Art
11 West 53 Street New York NY 10019
www.moma.org

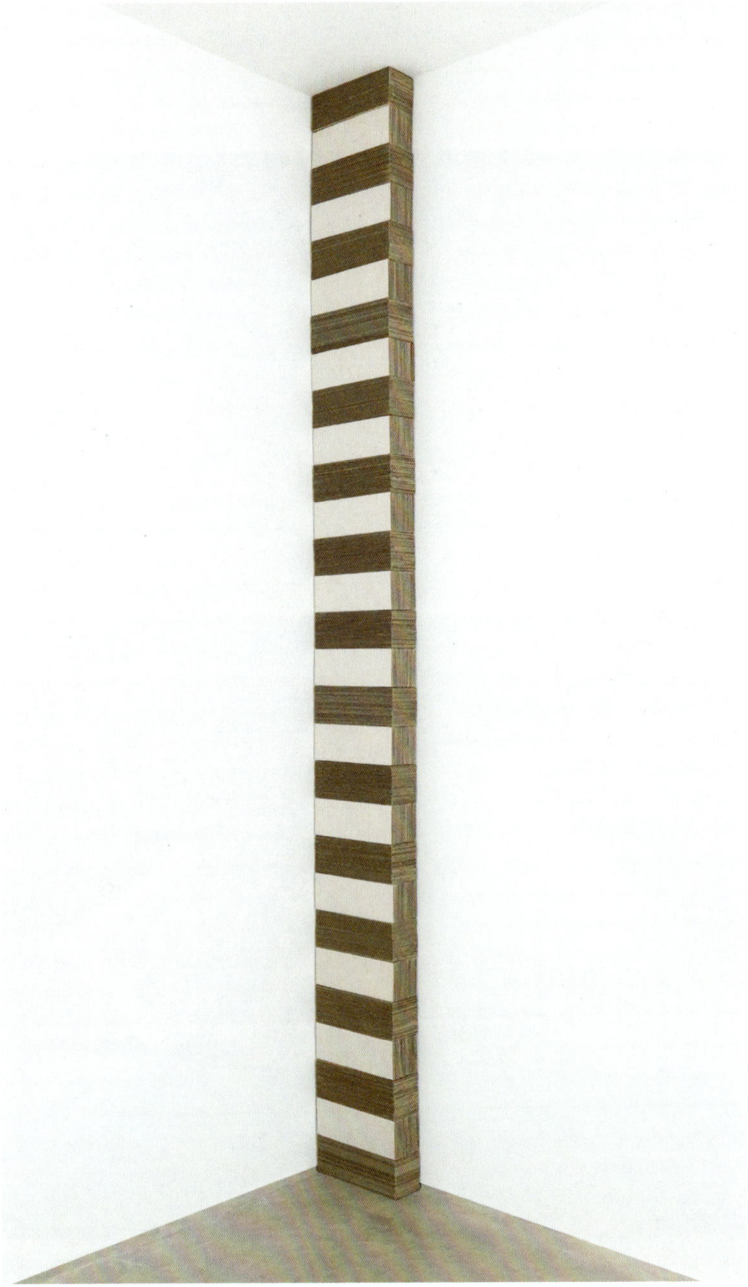

Lesley Foxcroft
Untitled (Vertical Cardstack), 1991

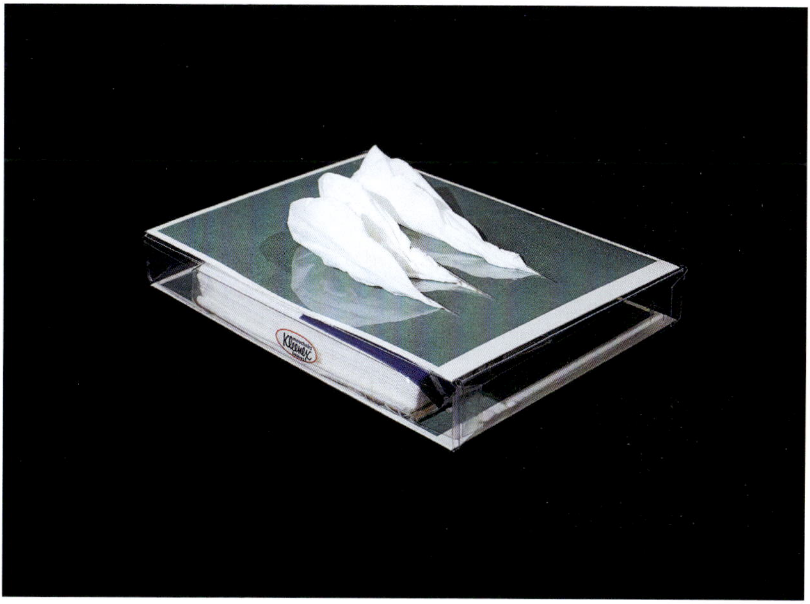

General Idea
Gesundheit (Why Not Sneeze Lucio Fontana?), 1991

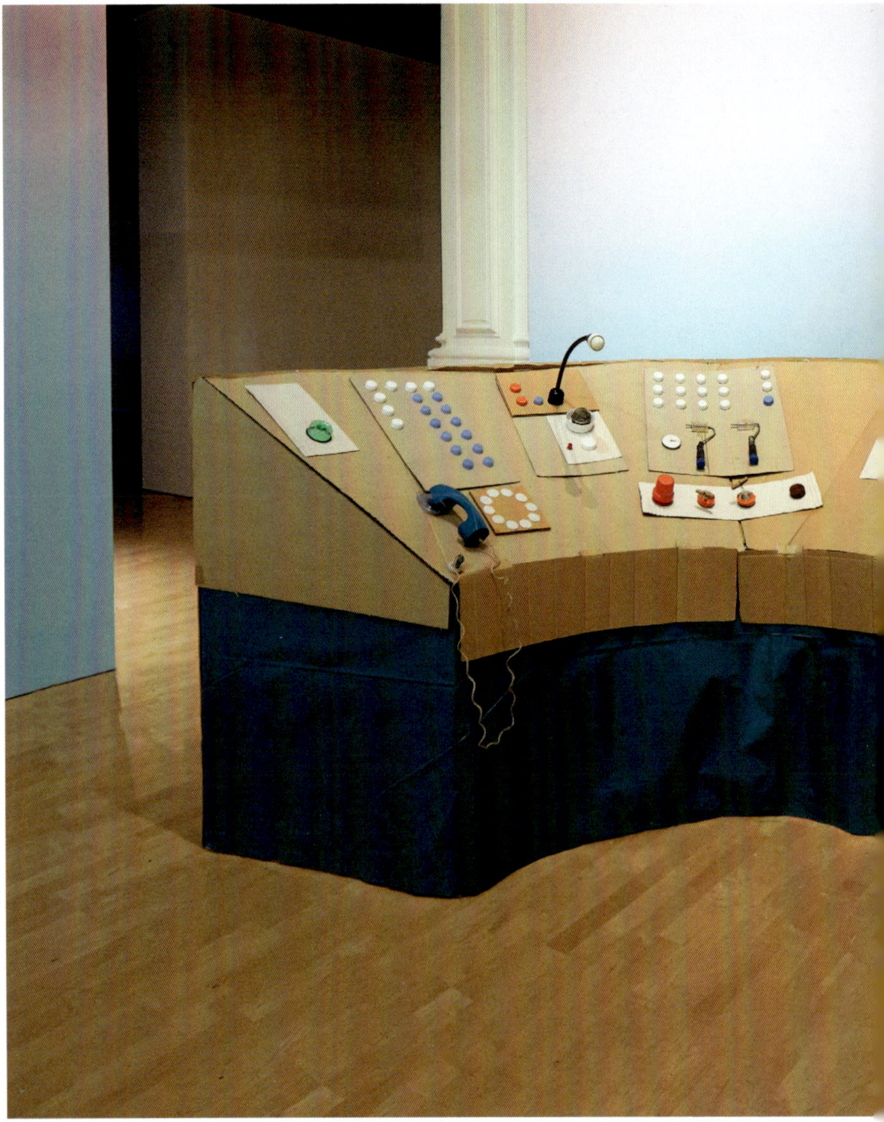

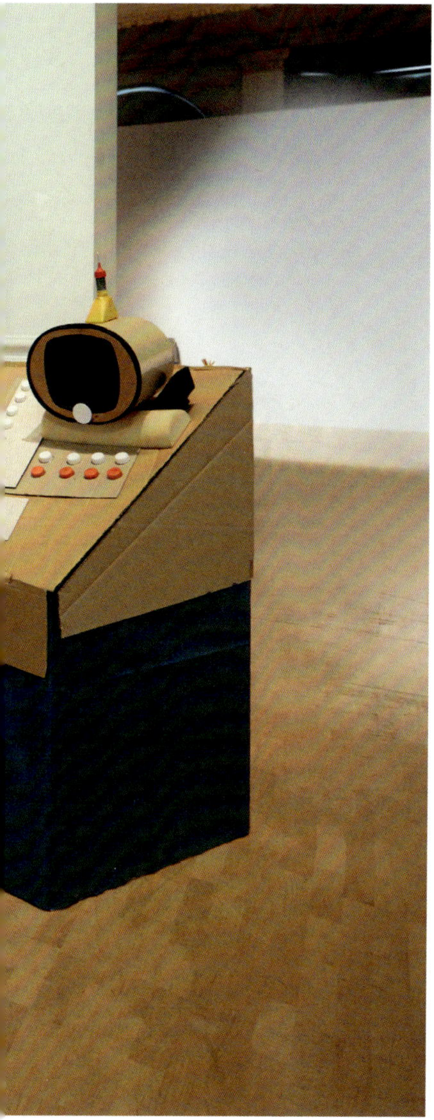

Brian Griffiths
Ron, 1996

Brian Griffiths is interested in how 'we make ourselves and re-make ourselves by the objects we surround ourselves with'. An obsessive collector, Griffiths's studio is full of cultural ephemera, bric-a-brac and furniture from the recent past, which he uses as a starting point for his idiosyncratic sculptures and installations. Through collecting and classifying, Griffiths says that 'you start to notice the strangeness of some objects in the world which you don't usually notice because the world's a noisy place'.

Ron is one of the numerous giant cardboard computers for which Griffiths is perhaps best known. Built out of sheets of corrugated cardboard, sticky tape, recycled bottle tops and plastic containers, his computers recall a childhood approach to model-making, in which rudimentary constructions have the potential to transport us to imaginary worlds. Griffiths's computers also reference the melancholic futurism found in low budget sci-fi B-movies, with flimsy sets and outmoded special effects that never quite manage to live up to our expectations.

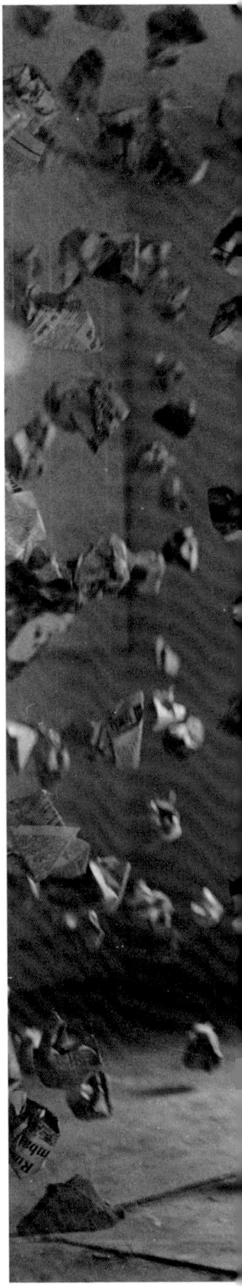

John Hilliard
765 Paper Balls, 1969

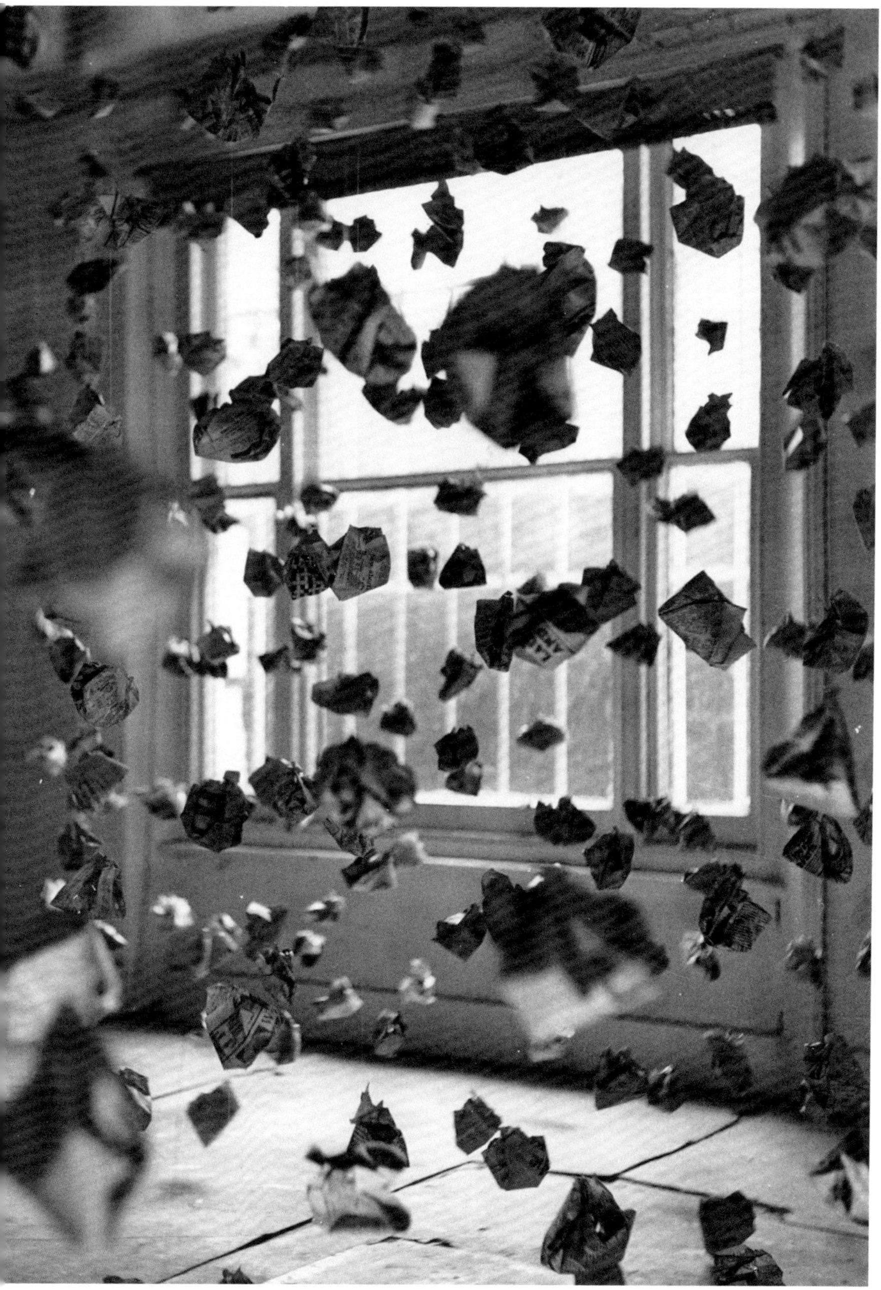

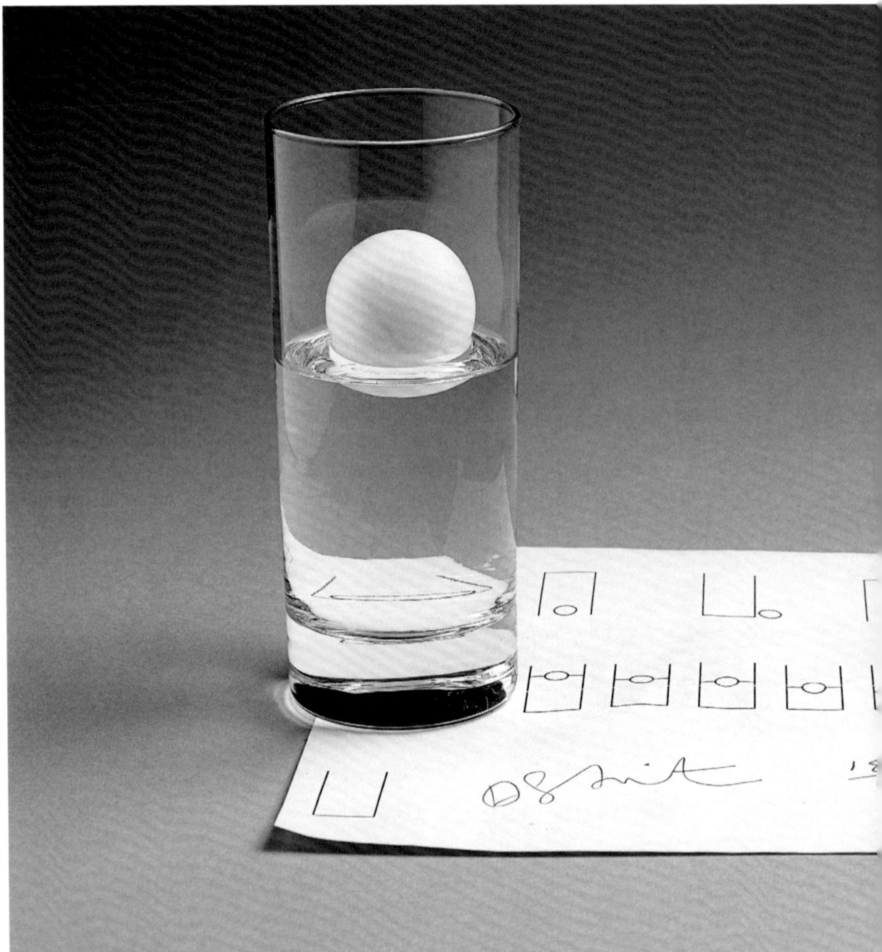

Damien Hirst
Relationships, 1991

Damien Hirst is internationally recognised for playful and often shocking works which explore enduring themes concerning love, life and death: from cows and calves suspended in formaldehyde, to the life cycle of a fly displayed in real time for all to see in a glass vitrine. One of his early works includes *I Want to Spend the Rest of My Life Everywhere, with Everyone, One to One, Always, Forever, Now* (1991), which features a ping-pong ball suspended in space above a simple glass structure, using a precise jet of air.

Relationships – a multiple produced in an edition of 125 – comprises a drinking glass, a ping-pong ball and a certificate that illustrates how, with the addition of varying quantities of water, the work can be presented in a number of different scenarios or material 'relationships'. In many ways, *Relationships* could be viewed as a miniaturisation of Hirst's major installations – a micro-drama in a mini glass vitrine, animated through the natural forces.

Gareth Jones
Cape, 1995

Cape offers a playful response to humble, everyday materials. It is also the outcome of a performance that reflected on youth, hope, heroism and the passage of time. As the artist explained:

'I'd bought a packet of number tickets from my local newsagent. They were the kind used in cloakrooms and tombolas. I was 29 and playing with the idea of my age, laying out tickets 1–29 and thinking about the future. At the same time I was thinking about a cape I used to dress up in as a child, and the cape wearers I'd been drawn to subsequently in my life. So I abandoned tickets 1–29 and stuck down all my future possible ages on a large piece of card that was to hand, and then threaded a piece of string through each end. I did this while watching a film on TV: *The Life and Death of Colonel Blimp* by Michael Powell and Emeric Pressburger, a powerful and controversial film made at the height of Second World War that is a plea for tolerance towards the enemy. Having finished making the cape, I put it on and watched the rest of the film.'

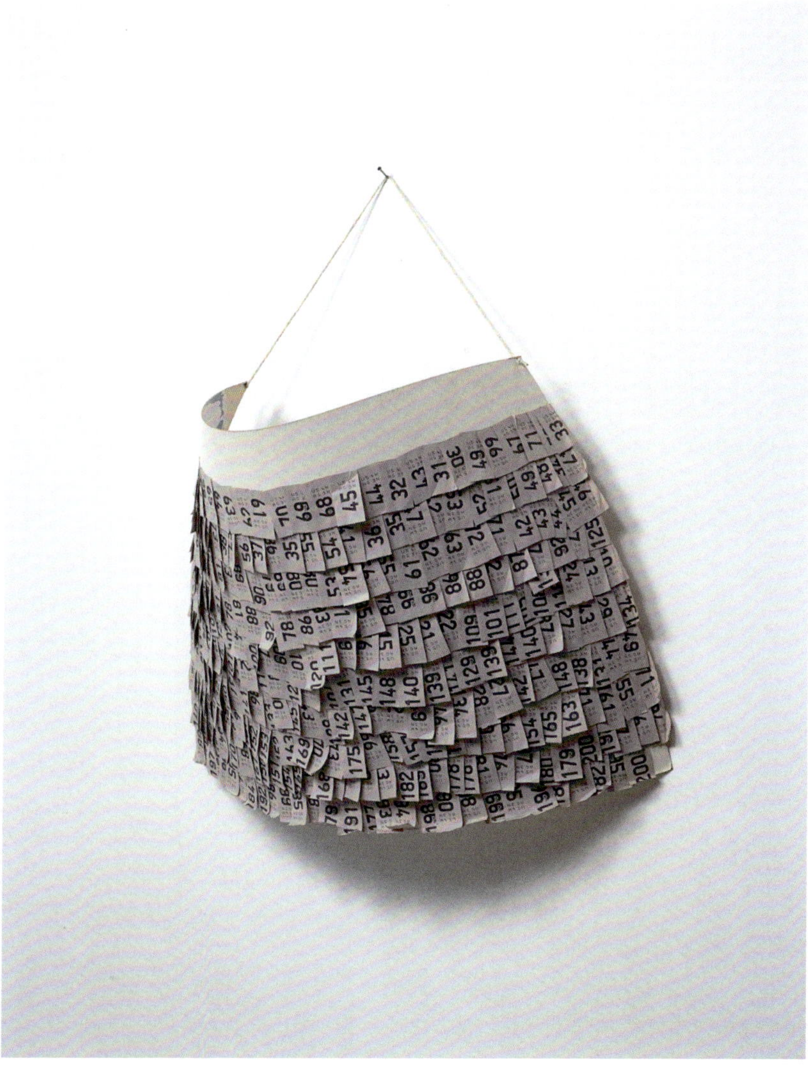

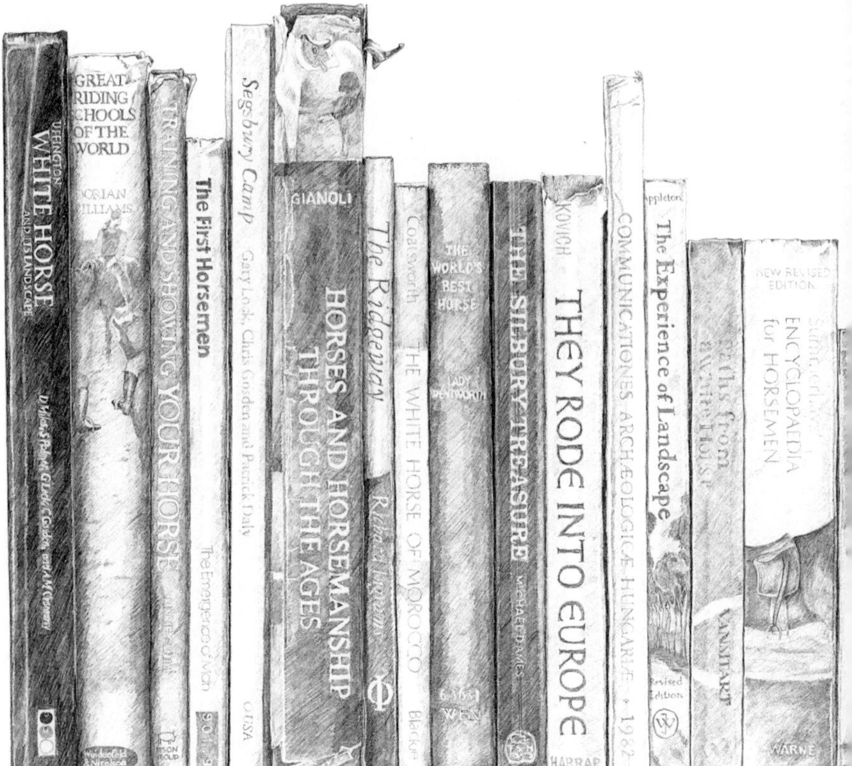
UFFINGTON
WHITE HORSE
AND ITS LANDSCAPE
GREAT RIDING SCHOOLS OF THE WORLD
Weidenfeld & Nicolson
TRAINING AND SHOWING YOUR HORSE
The First Horsemen
The Emergence of Man
Segsbury Camp
Gary Lock, Chris Gosden and Patrick Daly
GIANOLI
HORSES AND HORSEMANSHIP THROUGH THE AGES
The Ridgeway
Coatsworth
THE WHITE HORSE OF MOROCCO
Blackie
THE WORLD'S BEST HORSE
LADY WENTWORTH
THE SILBURY TREASURE
MICHAEL DAMES
KOVICH
THEY RODE INTO EUROPE
HARRAP
COMMUNICATIONES ARCHÆOLOGICÆ HUNGARIÆ
1982
Appleton
The Experience of Landscape
Revised Edition
NEW REVISED EDITION
ENCYCLOPAEDIA for HORSEMEN
WARNE

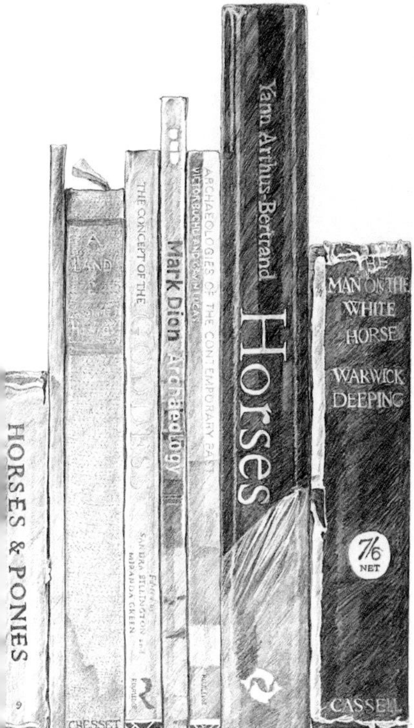

Tania Kovats
Books from the Museum of the White Horse Library, Non-Fiction, 2007

In 2006 Tania Kovats started a collaboration with the Ruskin School of Art and the School of Archaeology at the University of Oxford in order to gain an understanding of the conventions of drawing and recording archaeological finds. She then used these techniques to make a series of drawings in relation to the Uffington White Horse, a 3,000-year-old drawing carved into the chalk downland in southwest Oxfordshire. Together with her own drawings, Kovats assembled a collection of archaeological and vernacular artefacts relating to this monument, and horses more generally, and housed them in what she called the Museum of the White Horse, a converted horsebox that toured to various locations including hillsides and racecourses from August to December 2007. She referred to it as a 'travelling landscape museum' which explores 'our relationship with the horse as a symbolic and actual point of access into the landscape and the white horse as a mythical archetype'.

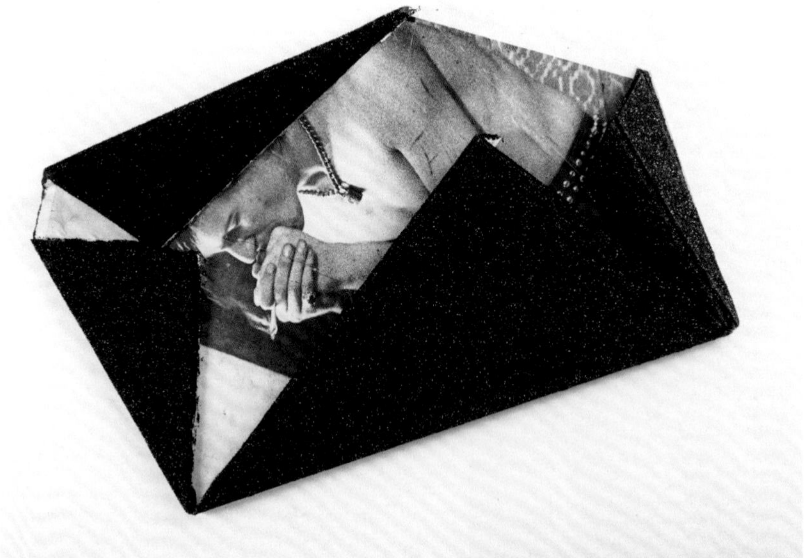

Jim Lambie
Sid Vicious, 2001

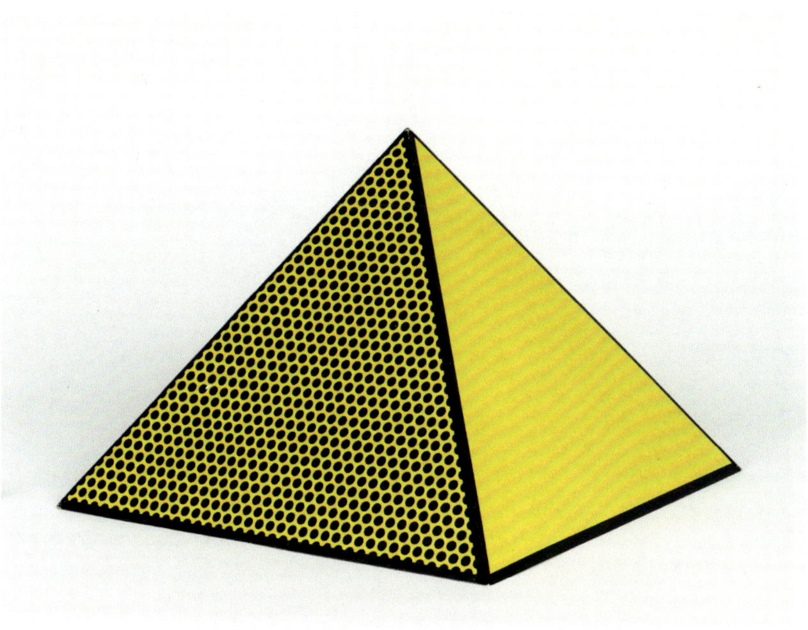

Roy Lichtenstein
Pyramid, 1968

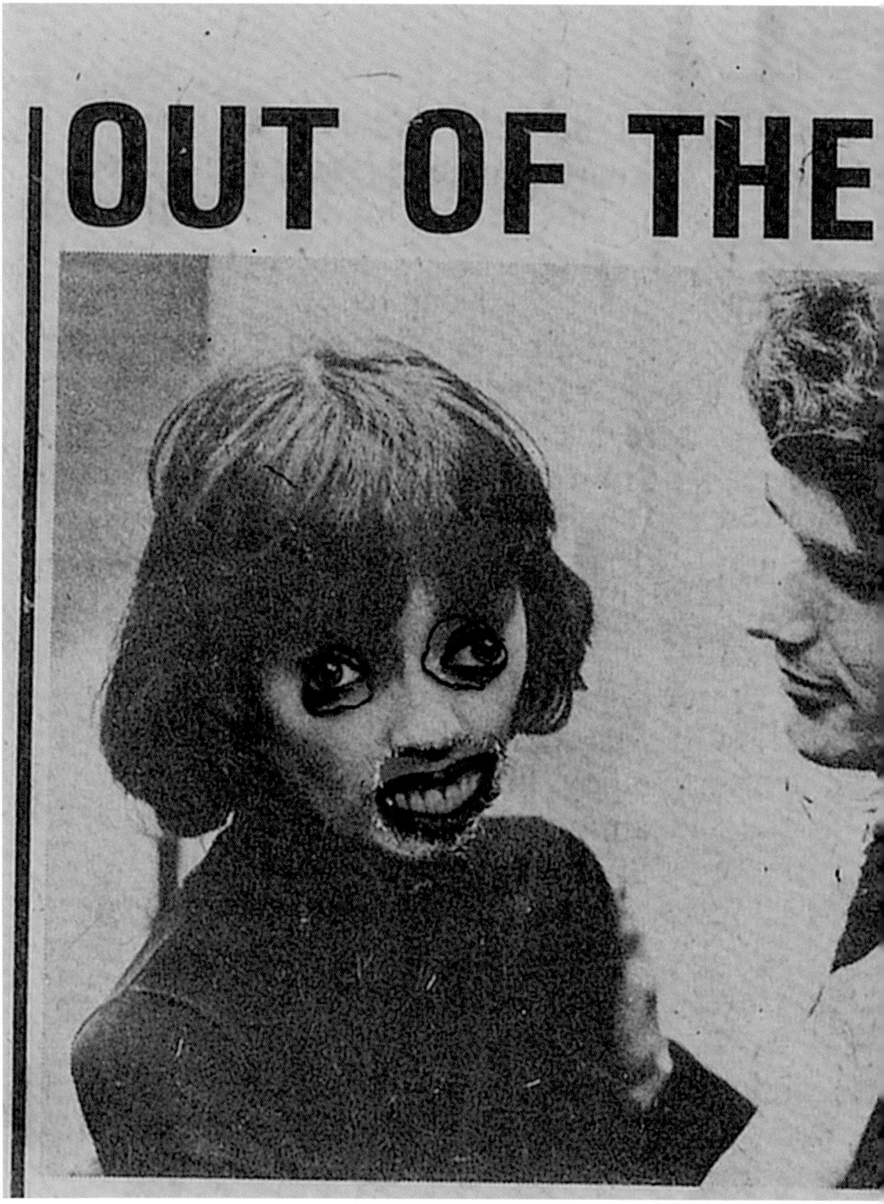

Linder
Untitled, 1977

BLUE

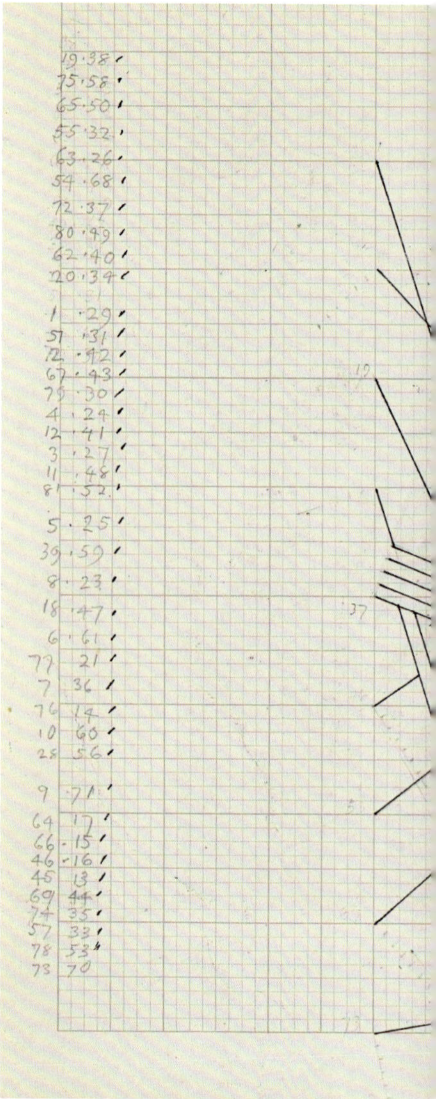

Kenneth Martin
Study for Chance, Order, Change 2 (Ultramarine Blue), 1976

Kenneth Martin's method of making sculptures and paintings was to evolve complex configurations according to simple rules and structures. He spent the last 15 years of his life working on a series of drawings and paintings titled *Chance and Order*. In these works, he started with a squared grid which was numbered around the edges. The numbers were then written on pieces of paper, put in an envelope and chosen at random. Each pair of numbers were joined on the grid to make a line, allowing a rhythm to develop. Martin would then decide on the length, scale and thickness of the line and its place in the order of sequence. Through this series, he came to realise that he could develop works with the use of chance; as he stated, they were: 'a sequence independent of my personality. I could be the spectator. Hence "Chance and Order". These works were not made by knowledge and erudition. All was discarded except a numbered field, the character of the activity of the drawing of lines, and my sense of art'.

This drawing is a study for the painting *Chance, Order, Change 2* (1976) which is also owned by the Arts Council Collection.

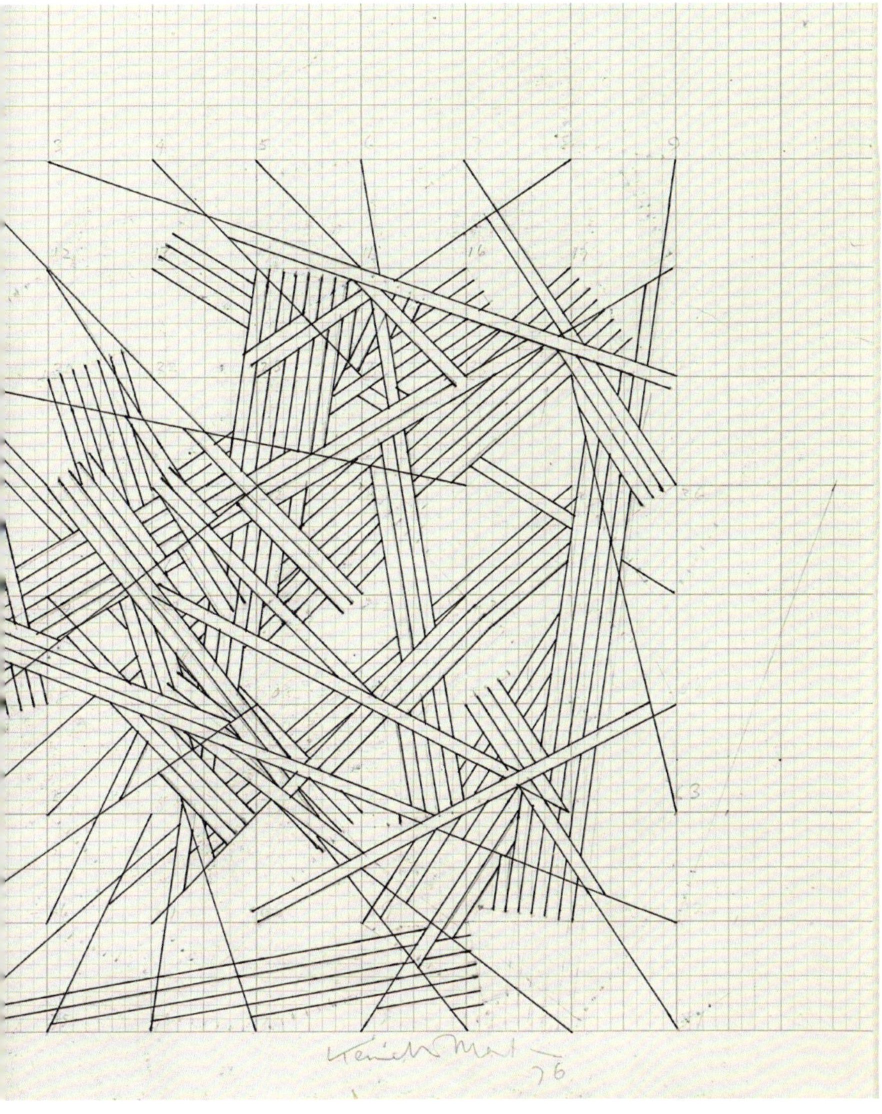

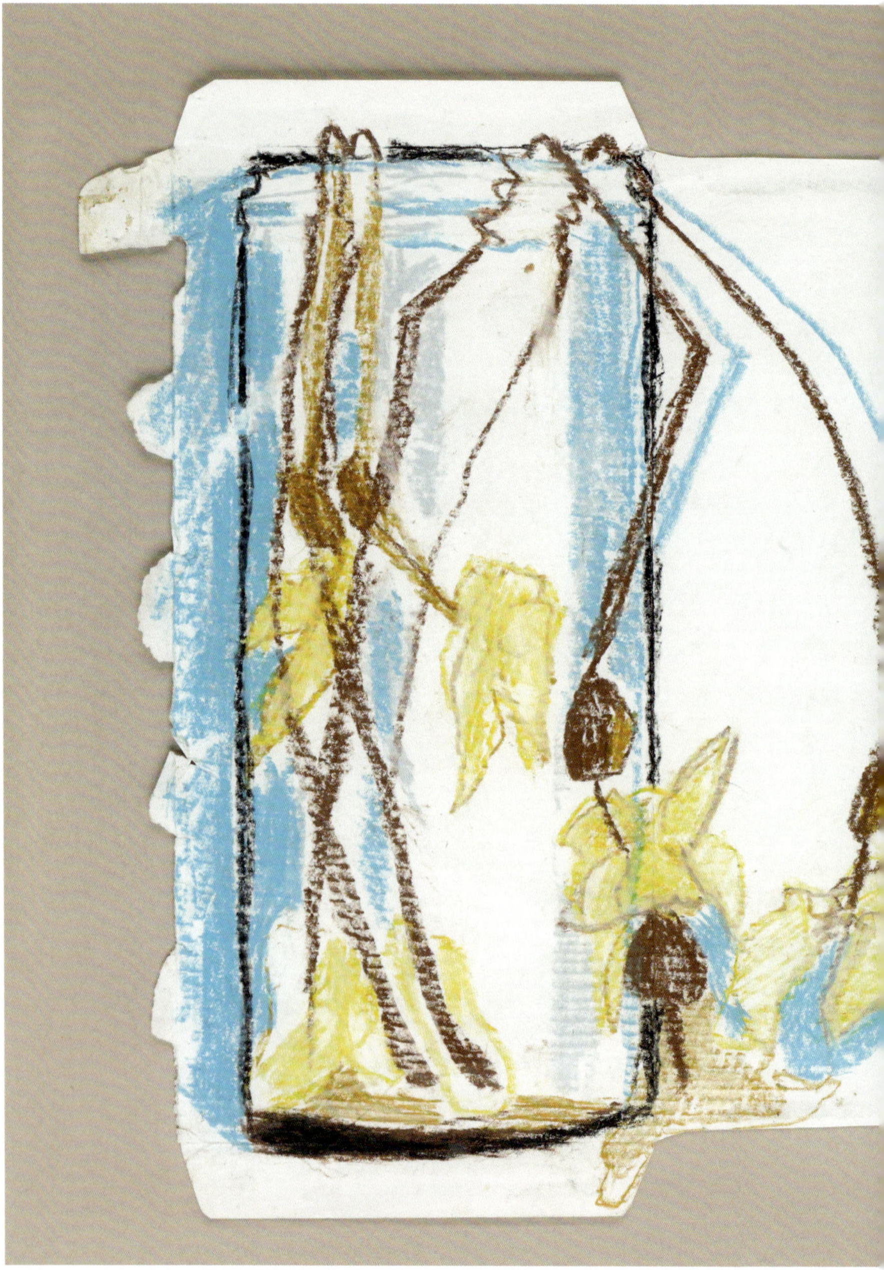

Margaret Mellis
Dying Daffodils, 1989

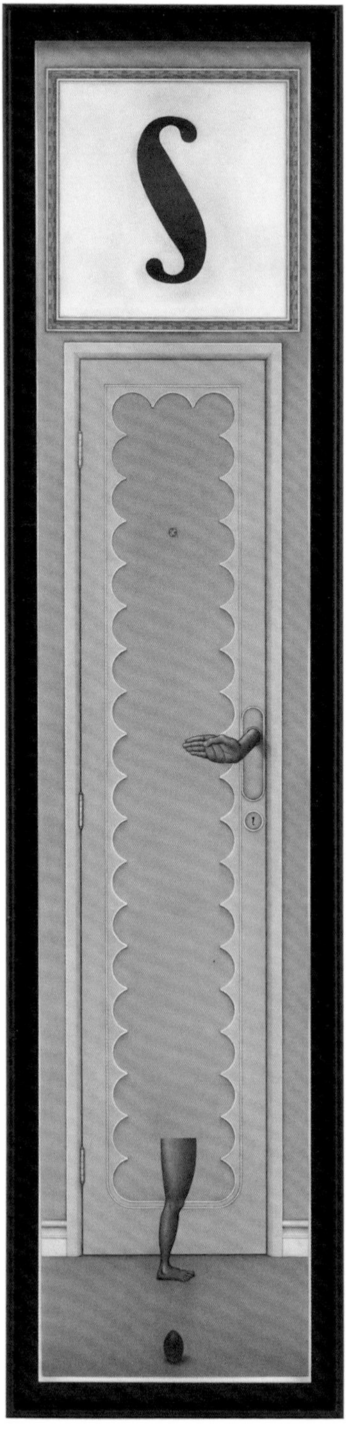

Paul Noble
Large S, 2015

Paul Noble is best known for his large, intricate graphite drawings of surreal urban settings, including those from his major drawing project *Nobson Newtown*. These meticulous drawings of a fantastic sprawling metropolis were produced over the course of two decades using the method 'cavalier projection', a cartographical method which collapses the distinction between the foreground, midground and background to create an image deliberately lacking in depth. The artist grew up on the north-east coast of England, and claims to 'think like the flat, grey skies of wintery Whitley Bay'.

Since 2015, Noble's drawings have presented flat interiors encased within wooden frames designed by the artist, with the suggestion that his drawings can also be sculptures. In *Large S* a miniature bare leg detached from its owner stands sentry outside a tall, ornate door whose handle has morphed into a hand, raised as if to gesture 'no entry'. The limb, accompanied by a solitary egg, appears to wait patiently in this surreal space, which calls to mind a shrunken Alice trying to navigate Wonderland, as well as the unfortunate characters that populate the works of Hieronymus Bosch.

Eduardo Paolozzi
A Logical Picture of Facts is a Thought (3) Tractatus '21-22', 1994

Eduardo Paolozzi frequently referred back to his earlier works and in this collage he returns to the subject of the Viennese philosopher Ludwig Wittgenstein (1889–1951), who is shown here, and was the subject of Paolozzi's *As Is When* screenprints of 1964–65. As well as being intrigued by the idea of linking art and philosophy, Paolozzi, who was born in Leith to Italian parents, identified with Wittgenstein's feeling of being an outsider in Britain. The title refers to *Tractatus Logico-Philosophicus*, which Wittgenstein wrote while serving in the Austrian army during the First World War.

The artist Richard Hamilton perceptively noted that the whole of Paolozzi's work comes out of the techniques and ideas of collage: 'you tend to break it apart before you put it together again'. Here Paolozzi returns to deconstructing and reconstructing Wittgenstein's head by collaging together magazine printed photographs from Derek Jarman's 1993 *Wittgenstein* film with those of the philosopher and parts of ancient Greek statues.

This collage was made for a screenprint of the same title which was part of Paolozzi's commemorative portfolio for the quincentenary of Jesus College, Cambridge. Wittgenstein had strong connections to Cambridge, both studying there and later being appointed Chair of Philosophy.

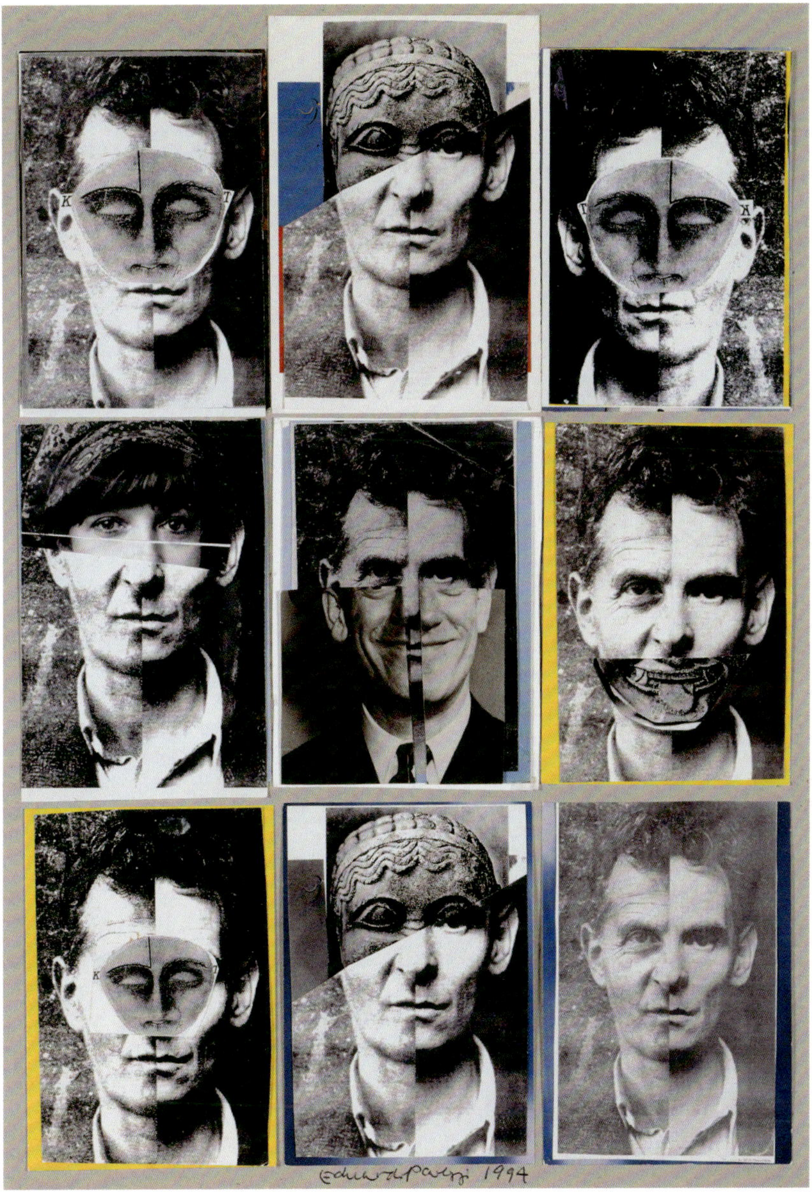
Eduardo Paolozzi 1994

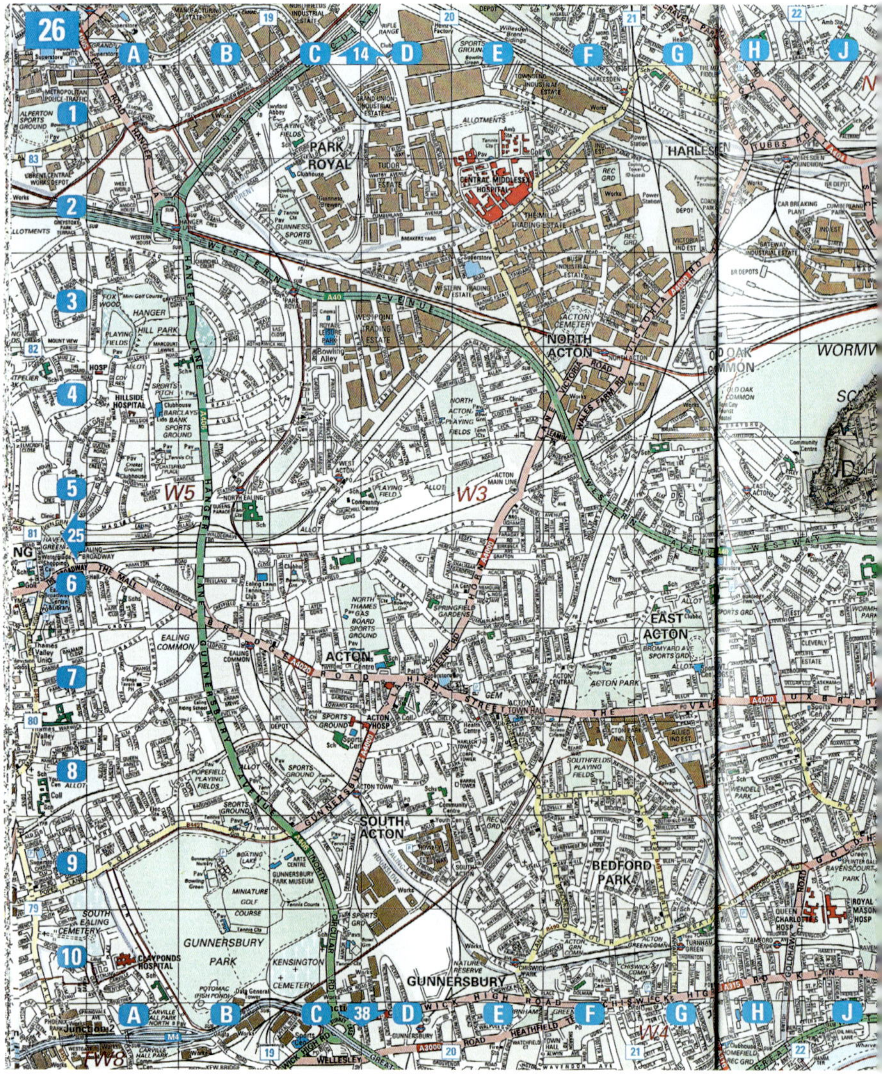
PARK ROYAL
HARLESDEN
NORTH ACTON
OLD OAK COMMON
WORMWOOD
HANGER HILL PARK
W5
W3
W4
W6
EALING COMMON
ACTON
EAST ACTON
SOUTH ACTON
BEDFORD PARK
GUNNERSBURY PARK
GUNNERSBURY
CENTRAL MIDDLESEX HOSPITAL
HILLSIDE HOSPITAL
CLAYPONDS HOSPITAL
SOUTH EALING CEMETERY
KENSINGTON CEMETERY
ACTON CEMETERY
ACTON PARK
WESTERN AVENUE
HANGER LANE
GUNNERSBURY LANE
NORTH CIRCULAR RD
UXBRIDGE ROAD
HIGH STREET
HORN LANE
VICTORIA ROAD
CHISWICK HIGH ROAD
THE MALL
WESTWAY
THE VALE
GOLDHAWK ROAD
QUEEN CHARLOTTES HOSP
ROYAL MASONIC HOSP
RAVENSCOURT PARK
Junction 2
M4
A40
A406
A4020
A4000
A3000
A315
A
B
C
D
E
F
G
H
J
1
2
3
4
5
6
7
8
9
10
14
38
25
19
20
21
22
79
80
81
82
83

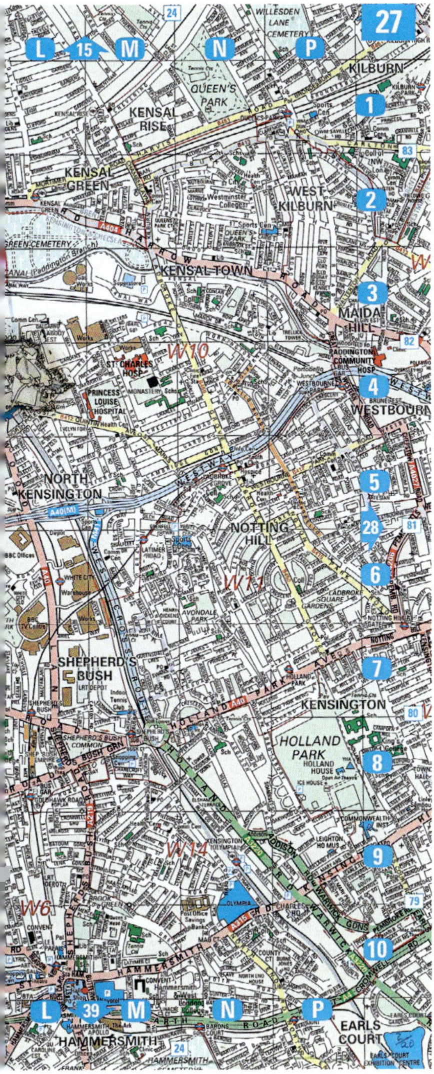

Cornelia Parker

Meteorite Lands on Wormwood Scrubs, 1998

Cornelia Parker has held a long-time fascination with meteorites and has investigated the possibility of one day sending a meteorite back into space. In anticipation of this event, she has created a series of prints depicting fictional landings on different parts of London, using a heated piece of a Gibeon meteorite, found in Namibia in 1836.

Destruction of objects using techniques including crushing, steamrolling and burning has been a feature of Parker's work. In this series, the meteorite is heated and then placed on an enlarged map of the city, burning its way through the paper, and leaving its imprint in some of London's most famous landmarks. The subsequent burns over locations such as Buckingham Palace, St Paul's Cathedral, the Houses of Parliament and Wormwood Scrubs, echo craters left by giant meteorites as they fall to earth and mark the spot where the everyday meets the extraterrestrial. As Parker says, 'an alien object from space, the meteorite, embodies fear of the unknown, fear of the future. In this sense this is an apocalyptic work for the end of the millennium.'

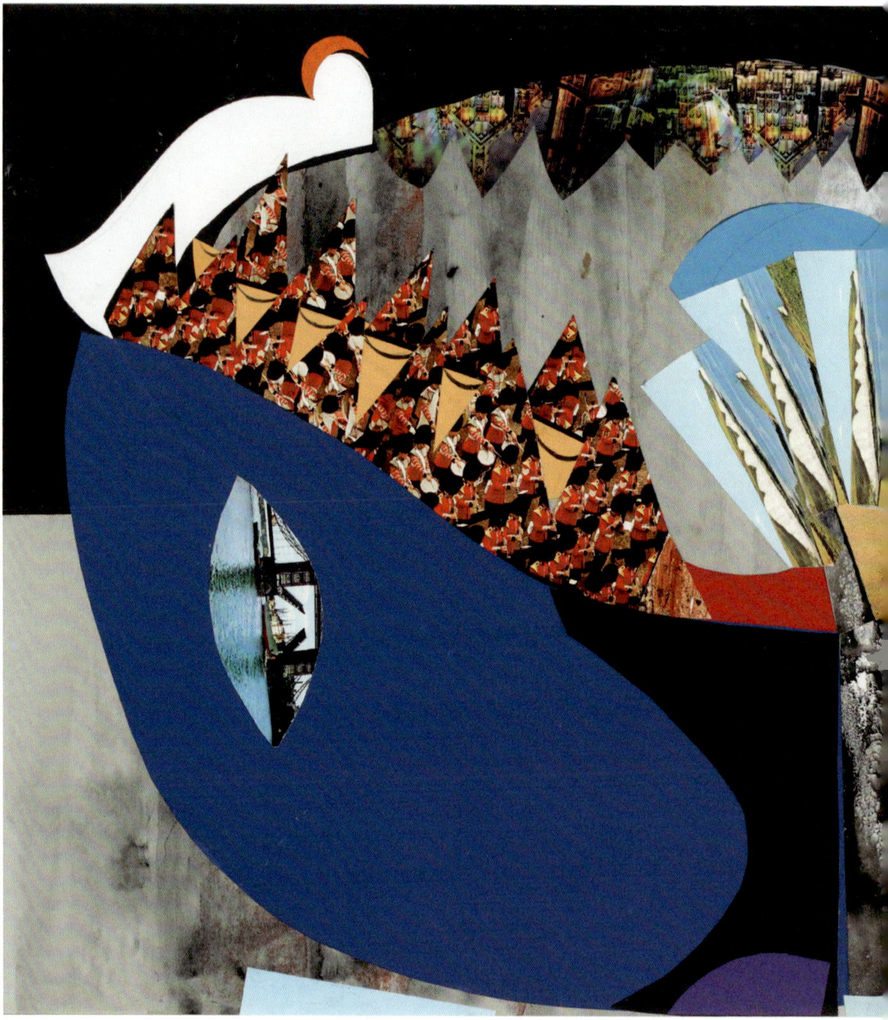

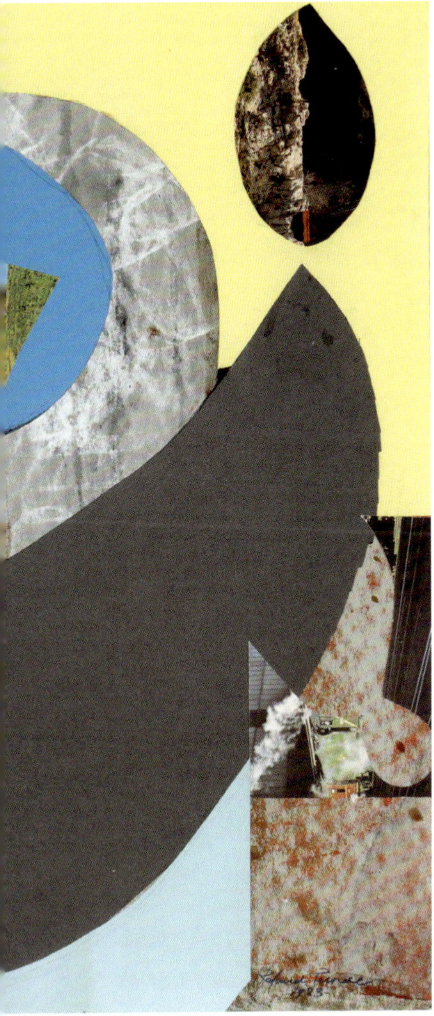

Roland Penrose
The Final Dictator, 1983

This is one of the last collages made by Roland Penrose in the year before he died. By 1983 the artist's mounting problems with his eyesight and loss of short-term memory had made it impossible to continue writing but by this time he had redirected his energy to making collages from picture postcards in a continuation of the style he established in 1937. He travelled widely from 1978 to his death in 1984 and this work reflects the different locations he visited during those years.

The Final Dictator was made in his studio at Farley Farm House in Sussex, and the images selected depict both local sights and London scenes. These include members of the Queen's Guard on parade, the white cliffs of the Seven Sisters and Tower Bridge. The plain areas are coloured paper cuttings, as well as paper pieces prepared with charcoal and decalcomania, typical of his studio work from this period.

The title *The Final Dictator* probably stems from Penrose's thoughts of his own death. During his lifetime he had opposed Franco, Mussolini and Hitler, and now he was facing the ultimate dictator with similar fearlessness.

A recurrent motif in his late works is the use of shapes resembling vertically mounted lips, which appear here on the upper right and middle left. The lips of Penrose's late wife, Lee Miller, were immortalised by Man Ray in his painting *Observatory Time: The Lovers* (1932–34). Penrose took this form and tilted it vertically, alluding to the representation of female genitalia. From the mid 1940s, Penrose used these as an allegory for Miller's presence; in his late-period works, however, the same motif reoccurs as if signifying his ultimate destination. Penrose died on Miller's birthday, 23 April 1984.

Simon Periton
SP, 1995

Simon Periton creates delicate paper cut-outs, or doilies, with a subversive edge. He takes inspiration from a range of sources, including popular culture, nature and politics. Doilies are often linked with the twee and old-fashioned, but Periton's pieces overturn this notion with their vibrant colour palette and social critique. 'When I first started doing the doilies, it was like revisiting childhood. Sitting at home on a rainy Sunday afternoon, with bits of paper folded into four, which I'd cut out and open up. I didn't really know what I was going to get until I opened them out... On the one hand it's about control, and on the other hand it's about what you can't control'.

SP was one of the earliest doily pieces that Periton made. It features the letters S and P, which are both his initials and those of the band Sex Pistols. The piece is an early example of Periton's fusion of punk imagery with the ornate. It also speaks of identity, a signature suspended within a decorative framework.

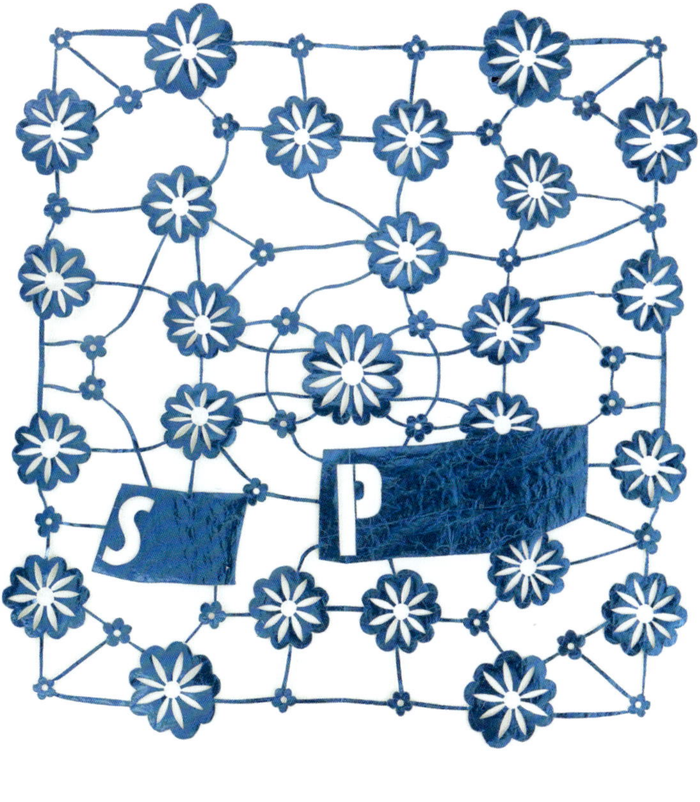
S
P

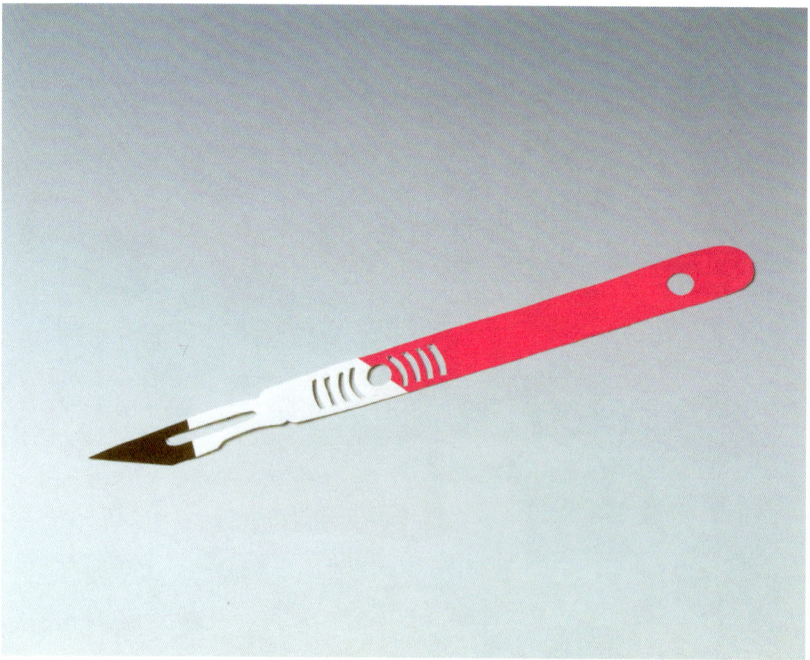

Simon Periton
Scalpel, 2000

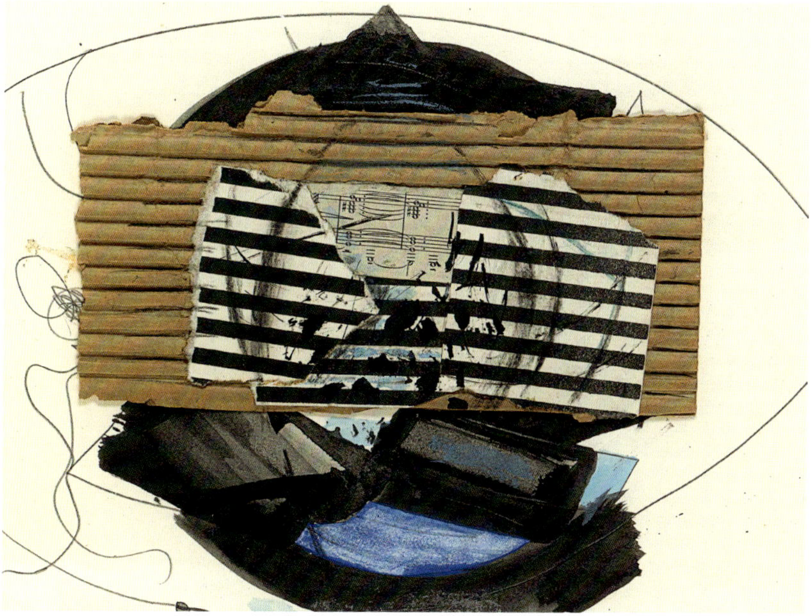

Ceri Richards
Music Theme, 1961

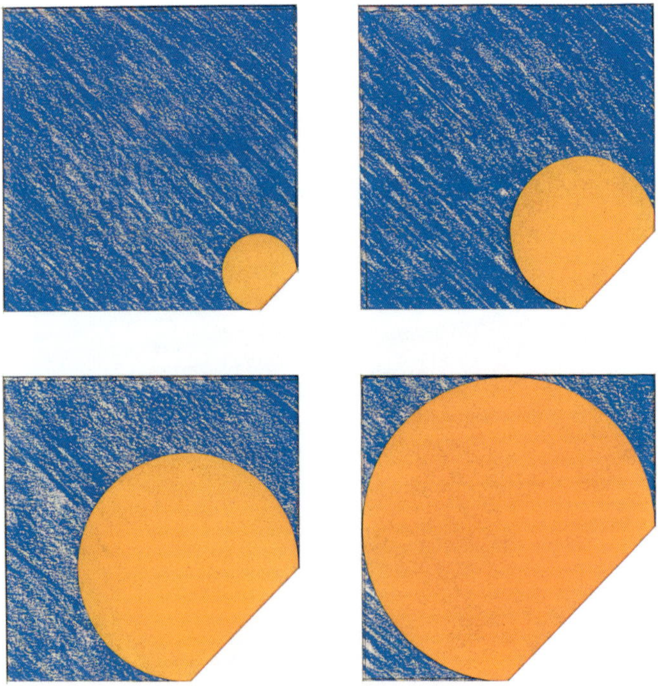

Richard Smith
Blue and Orange, 1966

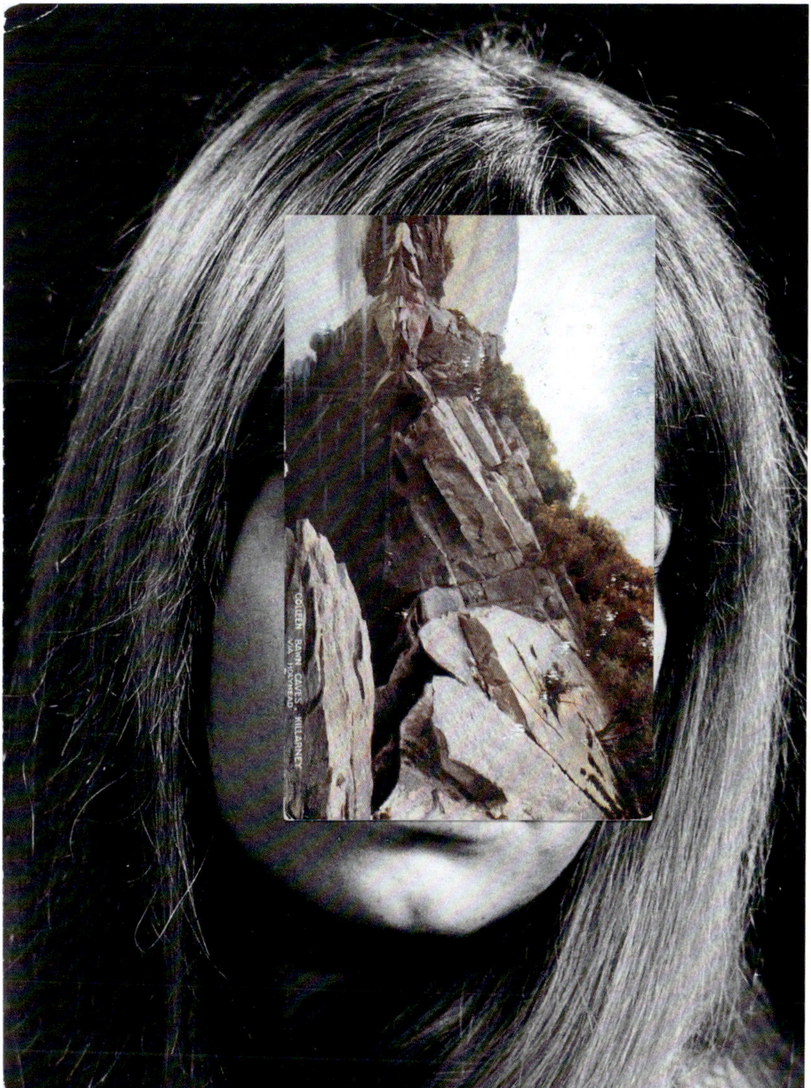

John Stezaker
Mask LXIV, 2007

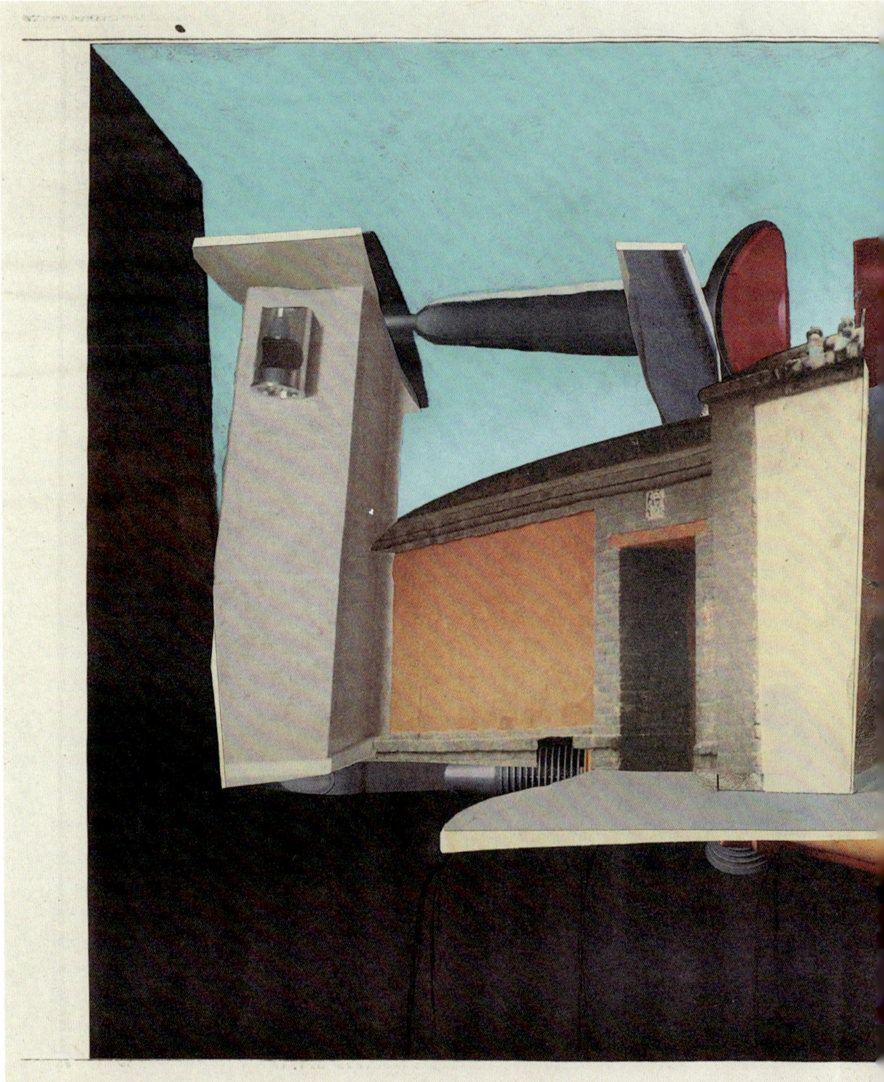

Tony Swain
In Baltimore You Think of Hats and Shoes, 2004

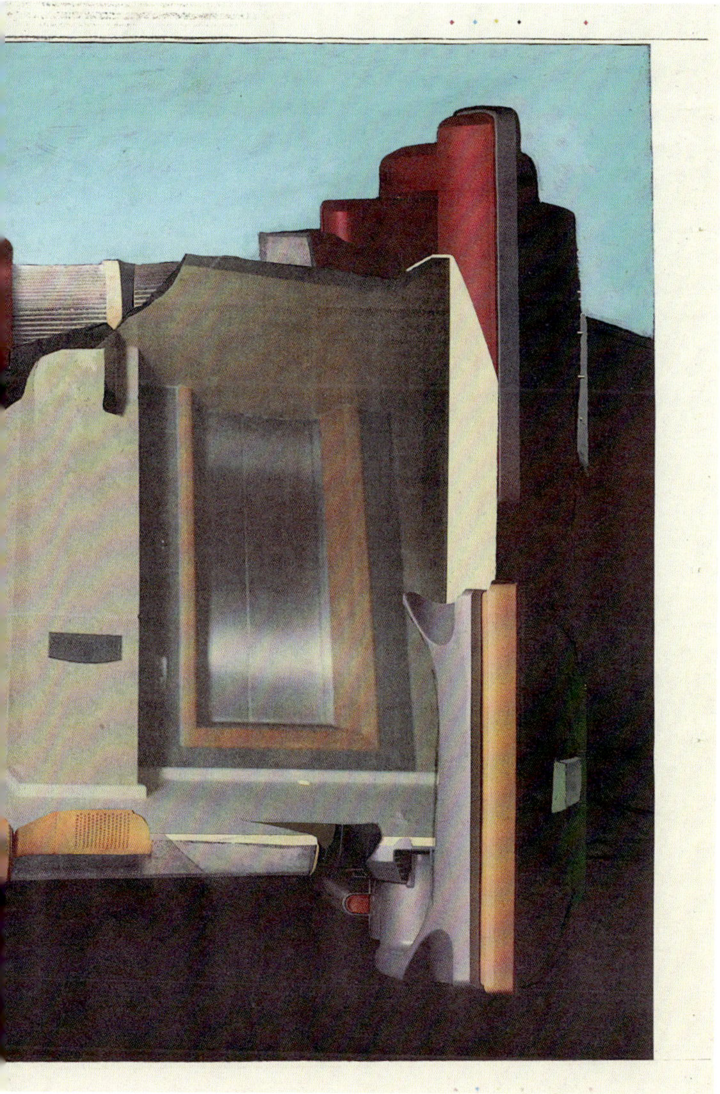

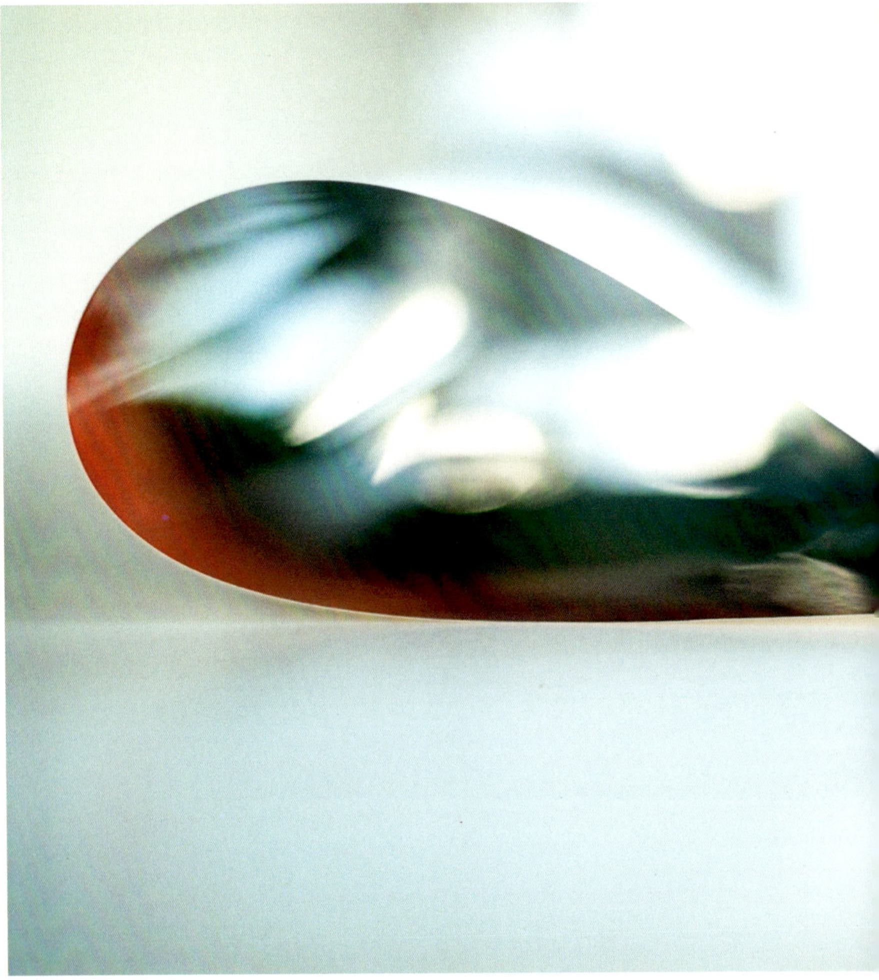

Wolfgang Tillmans
paper drop (London), 2008

The work of Wolfgang Tillmans is characterised by the artist's ongoing observation of his immediate surroundings and his investigations into the potential of the photographic medium. He composes arresting portraits, landscapes and still lifes, in which his subjects often appear transitory, as well as abstract works, which seem to have been created through impulsive gesture.

Paper is the material basis of almost all of Tillmans's work. The artist explains: 'I love the piece of paper itself, this lush, crisp thing. A piece of photographic paper has its own elegance, how it bows when you have it hanging in one hand or in two and manipulate it, expose it to light – I guess it is quite a gestural thing'. From 2000 onwards, he began to make pictures of glossy photographic paper, which he exposed to certain coloured light before processing it. In his work *paper drop (London)* we see a sheet of this paper, which has been folded backwards onto itself to form a tunnel. Light pours through, illuminating the void with incandescent red and blue tones, a fleeting moment of splendour.

List of Works

All works are Arts Council Collection, Southbank Centre, London, unless otherwise stated. All measurements are given in centimetres and are height × width × depth.

Roger Ackling (b. 1947; d. 2014) p. 25
Five Hour Cloud Drawing, 1980
Sunlight on card
62.4 × 75.2

Art & Language pp. 26–27
(Michael Baldwin, b. 1945;
Mel Ramsden, b. 1944)
Map to Not Indicate..., 1991
Cardboard
5.4 × 24.6 × 32.6

Gillian Ayres (b. 1930) p.28
Untitled, 1965
Mixed media on paper
48.3 × 69.9

Anna Barriball (b. 1972) p. 29
Window, 2002
Pencil on paper
55.5 × 51

Karla Black (b. 1972) pp. 30–31
Unused To, 2007
Sugar paper, chalk, polythene, toothpaste, nail varnish, hair gel and ribbon
Dimensions variable

Subtraction Isn't Wrong, 2011
Sugar paper, chalk, thread and eye shadow
72 × 60 × 14
British Council Collection

Derek Boshier (b. 1937) pp. 32–33
National Film Theatre, 2000
Graphite on paper
31 × 38

Ian Breakwell (b. 1943; d. 2005)
The Elusive State of Happiness, 1979
Newsprint and photograph on board
59 × 46

Tony Carter (b. 1943; d. 2016)
Remembering Landscape, 1974–77
Pencil and gouache on paper
65.3 × 53.6

Prunella Clough (b. 1919; d. 1999)
Vegetation, 1999
Ink on corrugated card
51.5 × 54.5

Jason Coburn (b. 1969)
Push the Button, 1996
Ink on paper
29.8 × 21

Tim Davies (b. 1960)
Untitled (Nail Drawing) No. 3, Part II, 1998
Scorched paper
122 × 122

Kate Davis (b. 1977) p. 35
Who is a Woman now? I, 2008
Pencil and screenprint on paper
160 × 129.5

Francis Davison (b. 1919; d. 1984)
Four Collages 4, 1979
Collage
80 × 89.5

Lesley Foxcroft (b. 1949) p. 36
Untitled (Vertical Cardstack), 1991
Corrugated cardboard
300 × 35 × 12, variable

General Idea (active 1969–94) p. 37
Gesundheit (Why Not Sneeze Lucio Fontana?), 1991
Ink, postcards, tissues and plastic box
1.9 × 10.8 × 15.2

Brian Griffiths (b. 1968) pp. 38–39
Ron, 1996
Cardboard boxes, plastic sheeting, plastic bottles, plastic tops, egg box, mop bucket, bin liner, golf ball, tea strainer, buttons, paint roller handles, foam, knitting needle, plastic pipe, cassette tape boxes, string and parcel tape
160 × 293 × 130

LIST OF WORKS

John Hilliard (b. 1945) pp. 40-41
765 Paper Balls, 1969
Photograph on hardboard
122 × 122

Damien Hirst (b. 1965) pp. 42-43
Relationships, 1991
Box, glass, water, ping-pong ball and certificate
21 × 25 × 14

Gary Hume (b. 1962)
Frankfurter Allgemeine, Le Monde, The Independent, International Herald Tribune, 1991
Printed paper and card
Three parts: 4 × 45 × 33,
one part: 4 × 36 × 26

Gwyther Irwin (b. 1931; d. 2008)
Midnight Hour, 1964
Collaged card on wood
99 × 55
British Council Collection

Gareth Jones (b. 1965) p. 45
Cape, 1995
Cardboard, string and paper
75 × 68 × 34

Ilya Kabakov (b. 1933)
Two Friends (for Parkett 34), 1992
Screenprint on card, plastic and paper
5 × 11.5 × 14.5

Tania Kovats (b. 1966) pp. 46-47
Books from the Museum of the White Horse Library, Non-Fiction, 2007
Pencil on paper
42.5 × 57

Jim Lambie (b. 1964) p. 48
Sid Vicious, 2001
Paper, board and glitter
43 × 60 × 20

Langlands & Bell
(Ben Langlands, b. 1955; Nikki Bell, b. 1959)
Uno City, 1992
from the *London* portfolio
Blind embossed print
71 × 74

Roy Lichtenstein (b. 1923; d. 1997) p. 49
Pyramid, 1968
Lithograph
35.4 × 50 × 50

Linder (b. 1954) pp. 50-51
Untitled, 1977
Collage
8.5 × 10.3

Richard Long (b. 1945)
River Avon Book, 1978
Book with mud on paper
1.4 × 14 × 16.4

Kenneth Martin (b. 1905; d. 1984) pp. 52-53
Study for Chance, Order, Change 2 (Ultramarine Blue), 1976
Pencil and ink on paper
26 × 34.5

Margaret Mellis (b. 1914; d. 2009) pp. 54-55
Dying Daffodils, 1989
Oil pastel on paper
25.2 × 23.4

Henry Mundy (b. 1919)
Untitled Drawing, 1982
Acrylic on paper
34.4 × 46.1

Paul Noble (b. 1963) p. 56
Large S, 2015
Pencil, paper and frame
263.2 × 65.6 × 8.4

Eduardo Paolozzi (b. 1924; d. 2005) p. 59
A Logical Picture of Facts is a Thought (3) Tractatus '21-22', 1994
Collage
48.5 × 34.1

Cornelia Parker (b. 1956) pp. 60-61
Meteorite Lands on Wormwood Scrubs, 1998
Printed and burnt paper
38 × 52

Roland Penrose (b. 1900; d. 1984) pp. 62-63
The Final Dictator, 1983
Collage
54.5 × 80

Simon Periton (b. 1964) p. 65
SP, 1995
Foil paper
55.9 × 53.3

Scalpel, 2000 p. 66
Coloured paper
16 × 1
British Council Collection

Ceri Richards (b. 1903; d. 1971) p. 67
Music Theme, 1961
Collage with pencil and wash on paper
26.7 × 35.6
British Council Collection

James Richards (b. 1984)
Rosebud, 2013
HD video
8 minutes 40 seconds

Bridget Riley (b. 1931)
Structural and Tonal Movements in Opposition, 1966
Pencil and gouache on paper
62.2 × 62.2

Jack Smith (b. 1928; d. 2011)
Sound Diagram with Paper Clips, 1975
Pencil, paper and metal
31.5 × 35.5

Richard Smith (b. 1931; d. 2016) p. 68
Blue and Orange, 1966
Pastel and collage
51.5 × 49

Sarah Staton (b. 1961)
Large Cigarette, 1991
Painted paper pulp
27 × 12 × 12
British Council Collection

John Stezaker (b. 1949) p. 69
Mask LXIV, 2007
Collage
25 × 18.5

Tony Swain (b. 1967) pp. 70–71
In Baltimore You Think of Hats and Shoes, 2004
Gouache and collage on newsprint
33.9 × 53.7

Harry Thubron (b. 1915; d. 1985)
Setenil, 1976
Framed collage and mixed media on board
112 × 127
British Council Collection

Wolfgang Tillmans (b. 1968) pp. 72–73
paper drop (London), 2008
C-print
54.3 × 64.3

Eleanor Wood (b. 1955)
Untitled 3, 1987
Watercolour and wax on paper
35.4 × 28.4

Published on the occasion of
the Arts Council Collection exhibition
On Paper

Perth Museum and Art Gallery
13 January – 3 March 2018

Gallery Oldham
17 March – 13 May 2018

Inverness Museum and Art Gallery
26 May – 14 July 2018

Oriel Wrecsam
28 July – 22 September 2018

Glynn Vivian Art Gallery, Swansea
29 September – 25 November 2018

Victoria Art Gallery, Bath
1 December 2018 – 17 February 2019

Thelma Hulbert Gallery, Honiton
23 February – 27 April 2019

Exhibition curated by Ann Jones,
assisted by Grace Beaumont, Kate Devine
and Louise Smith

Published in 2018 by
Hayward Gallery Publishing
Southbank Centre
Belvedere Road
London SE1 8XX, UK
www.southbankcentre.co.uk

Art Publisher: Rebecca Fortey
Project Manager: Diana Adell
Sales Manager: Alex Glen
Catalogue designed by ARPA Studio
Printed in UK by Pureprint

Short texts written by Grace Beaumont,
Rachel Graves, Ann Jones and Natalie Rudd

A catalogue record for this book
is available from the British Library.

ISBN 978 1 85332 355 3

Distributed in North America,
Central America and South America by
ARTBOOK | D.A.P.
75 Broad Street, Suite 630
New York, NY 10004
tel: +1 212 627 1999
www.artbook.com

Distributed in the UK and Europe
by Cornerhouse Publications
HOME, 2 Tony Wilson Place
Manchester, M15 4FN
tel: +44 (0)161 212 3466
www.cornerhousepublications.org

Front cover: John Stezaker, *Mask LXIV*, 2007

Arts Council
Collection